To Mangie

The Depth of
His Love

Love Juliet

The Depth of His Love

by

Tom Moye

Bridge-Logos *Publishers*

North Brunswick, NJ 08902

The Depth of His Love
by Tom Moye
ISBN: 0-88270-697-7
Library of Congress Catalog Card Number: 97-73691
Copyright ©1997 by Alfred Thomas Moye, Jr.

Published by:
Bridge-Logos *Publishers*
North Brunswick Corporate Center
1300 Airport Road, Suite E
North Brunswick, NJ 08902

Contents

Acknowledgments

I wish to thank all those who helped to make this work possible: my wonderful family, my wife and two daughters for their encouragement; my Mom and Dad who read the manuscript religiously for devotions for months; Sam Hardie who relayed a message from the Lord that I was supposed to be writing a book and confirmed the leading of the Holy Spirit; John Childs, and Rena Seals, without their computer knowledge this book would not exist; Al McLendon for his financial and spiritual support, and all those friends and family members who have enriched my walk with the Lord over the years.

Preface

The need for intimacy, to be one with another person, sharing our lives, our secrets, our pleasures and pain, is undoubtedly one of the great motivating forces for humanity. The desire for marriage and family suggests that we consider ourselves incomplete without someone else. Art, music, and literature are often expressions of reaching out to unite with others in a more than superficial way. Communication is an impetus in the recent explosion of technology. We group ourselves into gangs, communities, churches, and governments to eradicate loneliness. Yet, the pain persists. We feel like aliens on our own planet and search for ways to "join." In our desperation, sexual perversion, suicide, drugs and alcohol abuse seem like possible solutions. Divorce destroys our homes. We don't trust our government or our neighbor. We move further and further away from unity.

In contrast to this growing trend, we see a consistent theme of "oneness" in the Scriptures. Although God is three persons, He describes Himself this way, "Hear, O Israel: The Lord our God, the Lord is *one Lord*" (Deuteronomy 6:4, KJV), and Christ said, "I am *not alone*" (John 16:32). He told His disciples, "I and the Father are *one*" (John 10:30). Best of all, He said that we could be a part of this perfect communion. The seventeenth chapter of the Gospel of John is a prayer that all who believe in Jesus would "*be one*."

Separation and estrangement do have a solution in the person of our Savior. He promised, *"I will not leave you alone. I will come to you"* (John 14:18). "The Depth of His Love" is an attempt to make us, as believers, more aware of the intimacy to which our Lord is calling us. We no longer need to keep Creator God at arm's length like the Israelites at Mount Sinai, asking that He only speak through Moses. When we confess Him as "Lord," we're calling Him more than a military king. He is also Lord in the way Abraham was lord to Sarah, as husband, protector, and provider. The Scriptures show us clearly that the only way Jesus could be our Savior was to be "one with us," completely identifying Himself with us and our sin in the same way that two become one in a marriage (see Genesis 2:24).

What was accomplished on the Cross can hardly be considered a minor theme of Holy Writ. On the contrary, the primary preoccupation that pervades the Old and New Testaments is the Lord's great desire to be Husband to us. Thus He sought to provide everything for us "in the beginning" like a husband and sought companionship "in the cool of the day." The acts of God from the time of the Fall forward are best understood as His restoring the relationship lost in the Garden of Eden. At the culmination of earthly history described in the Revelation, we see the Bride descending from heaven in all her glory. Finally, God's plan is complete.

Seeing the Lord as our Husband moves the message "God is love" from abstraction to reality. All truths become relational, and we see our one purpose in life is to be His Bride. Christ "gave Himself up for . . . a glorious church," a Bride whose beauty reflects His own nature. My prayer is that these words will encourage you to be that Bride.

1
Is It True?

Since my childhood, I have heard believers described as "the Bride of Christ." I knew Paul's description of the husband-wife relationship concludes with the statement, "This mystery is great, but I am speaking with reference to Christ and the church" (Ephesians 5:32). I was even aware of the passage in Revelation 21:9 where an angel said, "Come here, I shall show you the bride, the wife of the Lamb."

Nevertheless, when a friend explained to me that "husband" was a title referring to the Lord and the Hebrew word for "lord" also meant "husband," I was doubtful. I confess, "Jesus is Husband" seemed too wonderful an interpretation for "Jesus is Lord." And yet, the phrase seemed to ring true. In my search for verification, I found

Scriptures that were well known to me and many more not as familiar lined up with this amazing revelation.

Under the Old Covenant, the Lord described Himself as "husband" to His people, "Your Maker is your husband, the Lord of hosts is His name" (Isaiah 54:5). In Jeremiah 3:14, the Lord says again, "For I am husband to you." Old Testament prophecies spoke of a time when the husband-wife relationship with the Lord, unfulfilled under the Old Covenant, would come to pass in the New Covenant. Hosea writes, by the Holy Spirit, "And it will come about in that day, declares the Lord, that you will call Me my husband" (Hosea 2:16). What Hosea predicted, Paul describes as realized in the coming of Christ and the New Covenant. In 2 Corinthians 11:2, Paul writes, "I betrothed you to one husband, . . . to Christ."

Husband and Provider

The Greek word translated as "husband" in the New Testament is *aneer*. The Septuagint (a Greek translation of the Old Testament made in the third century B.C.) uses *aneer* to translate the Hebrew words *bahgal* and *eesh* meaning respectively "lord, master, owner, husband" and "man, other half, steward, and husband."

For example, in 2 Samuel 11:26 we read that the wife of Uriah "mourned for her *husband*," and in Proverbs 31:28 concerning the excellent wife it reads, "her *husband* praises her." In both cases the Greek word used for "husband" is *aneer* (in the Hebrew, *bahgal*).

In Isaiah 1:3 we read these words, "An ox knows its owner, and a donkey its *master's* (Greek, *aneer*) manger, but Israel does not know, My people do not understand" (author's italics). The children of Israel *did not know where to be fed.* They did not realize that the Lord Himself was the source of their supply. As our Husband, the Lord is also our

Provider. There is simply nowhere else to go if we would be truly fed. This is what Jesus meant when He said, "I *AM* the bread of life" (John 6:48, author's italics). Jesus spoke of never being hungry again. Once we have found the ultimate bread and the perfect Provider, our insatiable hunger for sustenance is gone. We have found Him who satisfies.

Several passages are found in the Scriptures where *aneer* suggests not only the husband but the owner, "The one to whom it is due." The first of these is found in Exodus 22:8, "The *husband/owner* of the house," describing what a man is to do when a thief breaks into his house. A house is something very valuable to its owner, something to be looked after with jealous care. Shortly after my wife and I were married, I can remember locking the doors in our new home and making sure everything was secure for the night. There was a real sense of joy in doing this because it seemed to be part of the package of being a husband.

In John 10:10, Jesus warns us of the thief who steals, kills, and destroys. He then reassures us that He will not allow the thief to do his dirty work. Jesus will make sure we have the abundant life. The enemy wants to steal our joy, our peace, our assurance of salvation, and everything else of any real value in our lives; but he is powerless because Jesus, our Lord and Husband, is there to defend and protect His bride. In Luke 10:19, He tells us "Nothing shall by any means hurt you." Those are the words a husband would say to his bride if she were afraid at night.

Giving the Lord His Due

Proverbs 3:27 gives us the other side of the picture. "Do not withhold good from the *husbands/lords/those to whom it is due.*" Belonging always has two sides: privilege and responsibility. The Jews, under the Old Covenant, focused

3

on the privileges and ignored the responsibilities. As a result, the covenant relationship broke down. (*Covenant* is explained in chapter two.)

In the Lord's Prayer we acknowledge that certain things belong to the Lord, and we want to give Him what He is due. We say, "*Thine* is the kingdom, the power, and the glory (Matthew 6:13, author's italics). We are saying, "You're in charge. I am not. I give You the throne of my life as Your rightful place. If anything worthwhile is accomplished, it is by Your power and ability; and all the praise belongs to You instead of me." This attitude frees us from insisting on having our own way and building our own reputation to truly serve and glorify the Lord.

Destructive Husbands

The writer of Proverbs speaks wisely concerning the marriage relationship and belonging one to another. Proverbs 23:2, "A man *given to/mastered by (aneer)* desire" (author's italics). Proverbs 29:22, "A man *given to/mastered by (aneer)* anger" (author's italics). In each Scripture the person has a substitute husband that dominates their life, either anger or desire. Instead of giving themselves to the one true Husband who loves them more than He loves Himself and has their best interests at heart, they have yielded to other things that are destructive. These destructive husbands make slaves of them. We *will* be married to something. If we do not trust in the One who died for us, we will join ourselves to something or someone far less worthy and be mastered thereby.

Love, Trust, and Praise

The familiar passage found in Proverbs 31:10-31 concerning "the excellent wife," demonstrates how this matter of belonging is always one of love and trust and never one of force and fear. In verse 11 we are told, "Her *husband* trusts in her" (author's italics). At first this description seems backward, especially as we apply it to the Lord our Husband. Why should He trust in us, His Bride? Yet trust must always be mutual if there is to be a real relationship. Amazing as it may seem, the Lord really has entrusted us with everything He has. On one occasion Jesus told those who trusted in Him, "Father has chosen gladly to give you the kingdom" (Luke 12:32). The kingdom includes everything good that Father has for His Son. This faith is not so much in our ability to build the kingdom but in what the Lord can do through us as we continue to yield to Him.

Another expression of the husband's deep love for his wife is found in Proverbs 31:28, "Her *husband* . . . praises her." Perhaps this phrase also seems inappropriate when applied to the Lord our Husband. Yet the fact is, He does honor and praise us, His Bride. Psalm 8:5 says He crowns us "with glory and honor," and Psalm 23:5 pictures the Lord giving a banquet in our honor. In Revelation 21:9 we read the invitation, "Come here, I shall show you the bride, the wife of the Lamb."

The Lord in His Word often speaks of the glories of His Bride. He wants us to know how wonderful we really are, that we are worth His giving His life for us. If we, the church, could only see ourselves, and each other, as He sees us, we would be amazed at the glory yet "to be revealed" (see Romans 8:18). It would then be impossible for us to feel inferior or to look down upon any member of the Body of Christ.

The Lord, Our Conqueror

Aneer is also used in the Septuagint to translate *bahgal* in Isaiah 16:8, "The *husbands/lords* of the nations have trampled down its choice clusters" (author's italics). The reference is to conquering kings and princes who have overrun the vineyards of Sibmah. Few women want a wimp for a husband. They want a prince, a strong man they can admire. Such is the Prince of Peace. He brings peace by conquering His enemies so there's no more possibility of war. Then He conquers us with His love so that we gladly yield to the King of kings and follow Him with our whole heart.

No Longer Slaves

The other Hebrew word that corresponds to the Greek *aneer* is *eesh*, a more intimate term than *bahgal*. To understand the distinction we can see the two words contrasted in Hosea 2:16, "In that day . . . you will call Me *husband* (*eesh*) and will no longer call Me *master/owner* (*bahgal*)." The Lord is telling us that in the New Covenant ("in that day") we should think of Him more as a lover than a boss. Charles Wesley apparently caught the significance of this Scripture when he wrote, "Jesus, Lover of my soul, let me to Thy bosom fly." What is described here is the movement from Law to Grace, from duty to love. Jesus said to His disciples, "No longer do I call you slaves," and went on to explain how from then on He would be sharing His heart with those who believed in Him (see John 15:15).

The Lord, Our Completeness

When *aneer* (Greek) and *eesh* (Hebrew) are used together, they speak of companionship, belonging, and caring for each other. Genesis 15:10 gives us some insight into how absolute this belonging and joining really is: "Then he . . . cut them in two, and laid each *husband/half* (Hebrew *eesh*; Greek *aneer*) opposite the other." Abram had just cut the animals of sacrifice in two. There before him were the two halves of the same animal, each "husband" to the other. To make one whole animal required both halves. This is a picture of covenant and the husband-wife relationship. We often use the term "the better half" meaning "to make one whole person requires me *and my spouse.*" We are simply incomplete without them; they complement or compensate for our deficiencies.

How sadly lacking we are without the Lord our Husband! He is our righteousness, our wisdom, our strength, our joy, and our peace. Without Him we can do nothing (see John 15:5); with Him we can do anything (see Philippians 4:13). Until we are joined to Him, there is something terribly missing; we are not "whole" in any sense of the word. Once we are one with Him, we are complete (see Colossians 2:10); He is everything that is lacking in us.

The Lord, Our Companion

Along with completeness, we should find companionship in the marriage relationship. Husband and wife need to spend time together, to share life in each other's company. Leah was desperate for her husband, Jacob, to be a companion to her. At first, she could not have children; but once she began bearing him sons, she was certain Jacob would want to spend some time with her. She said, "Now . . . my husband will become *attached/ companion* to me" (Genesis 29:34, author's italics), and "Now my husband will *husband/dwell with* me" (Genesis 30:20, author's italics).

Jesus our Husband often expressed His desire for us to dwell with Him. He wants us to "abide," to live in His presence all of the time. (See John 15.) He has promised to be a companion to us, "I am with you always" (Matthew 28:20), and "I will *never* desert you, nor will I *ever* forsake you" (Hebrews 13:5, author's italics). Our Lord is not interested in giving us visitation rights on Sunday. He desires our walking

7

with Him every day, sharing life together, letting Him be our constant Companion.

The Lord, Our Steward

Most of us have heard of a "housewife," but the Bible refers to a "househusband" in Genesis 43:19. Speaking of Joseph's brothers, the Scripture says, "So they came near to the *husband of/steward over/man over (aneer)* Joseph's house" (author's italics). The steward was the man responsible for Joseph's house. He decided who entered and who did not, much like a butler today. Jesus our Husband, the Man "over us" as Lord, is responsible for the Church, His Bride. He does not want certain things to enter our lives, things like fear, doubt, worry, jealousy, and greed. Such things would be harmful to us. Because they lie outside the Lord's will for us, these things are called *sin*. One of the benefits of having Him as our Companion is His being with us constantly to guard against these harmful intruders.

A beautiful description of Jesus as the guard at the door of our life is found in Philippians 4:6-7, "Be anxious for nothing, but in everything by prayer and supplication with thanksgiving let your requests be made known to God, and the peace of God which surpasses all comprehension shall *guard* your hearts and your minds *in Christ Jesus*" (author's italics). As we share our life with our Companion through prayer, He is always there to guard our mind and heart, keeping out those thoughts and feelings that do not belong.

The Lord, Our Contractor

Another benefit of companionship is building a home together. The prophet Zechariah speaks by the Spirit concerning our Husband, "Behold, a *man/husband* whose name is Branch . . . He will build the temple of the Lord" (Zechariah 6:12, author's italics). Here Messiah ("Branch") is building Himself a house. A husband ordinarily provides a home for his wife and himself. So also does the Lord, our Husband, "I go to prepare a place for you" (John 14:2). If He wants us to dwell with Him, therefore He must provide us "a place" in which to dwell. (How He does is described in a later chapter.) The reason for this preparation is "that where I am, there you may be also" (John 14:3). He wants us to be in His presence.

The Lord, Our Perfect Husband

In the New Testament, *aneer* is translated as both "man" and "husband." The Perfect Man is also The Perfect Husband. The woman of Samaria had spent much of her life in search of "the perfect husband." She had already gone through five husbands, discarding one after another as unsatisfactory, and was working on another one. When Jesus said to her, "Go call your *husband*" (John 4:16, author's italics), He was deliberately pointing to the empty place in her life that only He could fill.

John the Baptist recognized the perfect Husband for the people of God. He cried out, "After me comes a *man/husband* (*aneer*) who has a higher rank than I" (John 1:30, author's italics). All of Israel had come out to join themselves to John through baptism, but he pointed to another Man, better than himself, to whom they, and we, should be joined. Later, Jesus was to refer to John as "the friend of the Bridegroom" (John 3:29). Christ Himself is the Bridegroom. As "the friend of the Bridegroom," John's function was to assist in bringing Bride and Bridegroom together, to "MAKE READY THE WAY OF THE LORD" (Matthew 3:3).

A Permanent Covenant

Once the Bride and Bridegroom have become one, by giving their lives to one another, their covenant is to be permanent. "If while her *husband* is living she is joined to another man, she shall be called an adulteress" (Romans 7:3, author's italics). The Lord desires faithfulness, not infidelity, from His Bride. The adulterer joins him or herself to more than one person at a time. Paralleling this with our relationship with the Lord, we would be trying to love Him and also love the world. Of course, this never works for very long. A person "married" to their job, sports, or a lover other than their marriage partner is a person headed for trouble. For this reason we are warned in Scripture, "Do not love the world, nor the things in the world" (1 John 2:15). Loving the world always takes away from our love for the Lord.

The Lord our Husband sought a faithful bride from the dawn of time. Adam and Eve, His original companions, were easily turned aside by what they saw with their eyes, the physical desire for food, and their wish to become like gods. After becoming the covenant people of God at Mount Sinai, the Israelites quickly reverted back to the gods of Egypt. Their history is one of repeatedly going after the idols of the nations surrounding them in Canaan. Even in the last days we are told "some will fall away from the faith" (1 Timothy 4:1). Is it any wonder that the one thing the Lord is looking for among His people is faithfulness? He defines a good servant as a "faithful" one (see Matthew 25:21), and instructs us, "Be faithful unto death, and I will give you the crown of life" (Revelation 2:10).

To be faithful is to be full of faith and love for the Lord. This fullness allows no room for love of lesser things that would turn us aside from our "first love" (see Revelation 2:4). We "live by faith" and "walk by faith," doing all that we do out of the trust and love we have for the Lord. (See Romans 1:17; 2 Corinthians 5:7.) Such faith and love cannot be turned aside once we have given ourselves without reservation to the Lord, allowing Him to truly become our Husband. That He wants to be our Husband is beyond question—He has expressed this desire in His Word over and over again. He only waits for a Bride to give Him her whole heart in order to have that longing fulfilled.

2

The Covenant With Abraham

The covenant agreement is introduced early in the Scriptures. After the flood, God made a covenant with Noah saying, "Never again shall the water become a flood to destroy all flesh" (Genesis 9:15), and He set His "bow in the cloud . . . for a sign of a covenant" (Genesis 9:13). Other covenants were to come later, including the covenant at Mount Sinai and God's covenant with David to give him an everlasting kingdom. The first picture of a full covenant relationship, however, is found in God's covenant with Abram. Paul points out that this covenant preceded and surpassed even the covenant at Sinai (see Galatians 3:17-18).

What Is a Covenant?

A covenant is a contract between two or more parties that is sealed with solemn vows. Political covenants usually involve pledges of mutual assistance and allegiance.

A covenant defines the terms of a relationship. Covenants between people signify the total giving of one's self to another. To symbolize this fact, participants exchange outer garments representative of who they are. They name all their assets and liabilities as if to say, "Everything that was mine is now yours as well." A sacrifice is made to bless the covenant. Next, a cut is made, normally, on each of the participant's wrists or hands, which are then bound together with cloth, cut-to-cut. (Abraham's covenant with God was symbolized by circumcision; modern Christian marriage covenants are sealed with a ring.) This is a symbol of the covenant makers giving of their lives to each other. Such blood covenants are forever, passed on from generation to generation. Then follows a covenant meal, depicting the fellowship to be enjoyed for years to come.

When God is offering covenant to man, it is never a contract between equals, but a sovereign act of grace—a King offering protection to his subjects. Promises are often made by the one initiating the agreement with corresponding obligations for the recipient. These promises, once made, cannot be broken.

God's Covenant With Abram

The outstanding example of covenant in our society is the covenant of marriage. Two becoming one—inseparable—this is the true meaning of covenant. When the Lord called Abram, He was actually calling for a bride. Out of all the people on earth, God chose Abram much as we choose a mate out of all the people we know. Best of all, when He chose Abram, He was also choosing us. This covenant was not only with Abram but with all his descendants as well. Galatians 3:7 tells us, "Those who are of faith . . . are sons of Abraham." The covenant was with Abram and "his seed" (see Galatians 3:16), which Paul points out is a specific reference to Christ. If we are *in Christ*, then the covenant is just as surely with us as if we had been there in the flesh with Abram and had sacrificed the animals along with him.

The Lord's original invitation to covenant with Abram is found in Genesis 12:1, "Now the Lord said to Abram, 'Go forth from your country, and from your relatives, and from your father's house to the land which I will show you.'" This passage sounds a great deal like a proposal of marriage when a man asks the woman he loves to leave home and family to live with him. In Genesis 2:24, we are told that marriage involves leaving father and mother, clinging steadfastly to the one we love most in the world so that we two become one flesh, "For this cause a man shall leave his father and his mother, and shall cleave to his wife; and they shall become one flesh."

Such a proposal doesn't usually take place at the first meeting even between those who are later to marry. Ordinarily it is preceded by a time of dating when the man and woman involved can get to know one another better. The Lord, however, doesn't need to get to know us better. He knows everything there is to know about us; and yet, in spite of this fact, He still issues His invitation. He knew all of Abram's shortcomings, but He called him anyway! He knows all of our shortcomings, and calls us yet today!

How the Lord could have such personal knowledge of Abram and us is not difficult to understand—He is omniscient. But how could Abram know the Lord well enough at this initial encounter to leave everything he'd ever known? This knowledge seems to have been instantaneous and almost absolute, the kind that can only occur with revelation. This is not knowledge of the intellect acquired through experience and deduction over a period of years. This is God opening the curtain on Himself so we see Him as He really is. The same type of instant intimacy took place with Moses at the burning bush where God revealed Himself as I AM. From that point on Moses knew God!

Like Father, Like Son

In the New Testament we see Jesus, our Lord and Husband, giving the same type of invitation. When asked, "What shall I do to inherit eternal life?" (Mark 10:17), He says to someone He has never seen before, as far as we know, "Sell all you possess . . . and come, follow Me" (Mark 10:21). Later, Jesus was to define eternal life as knowing Him in a personal way, becoming one in union with Him:

And this is eternal life, that they may know Thee, the only true God, and Jesus Christ whom Thou hast sent.

And I am no more in the world; and yet they themselves are in the world, and I come to Thee. Holy Father, keep them in Thy name, the name which Thou hast given Me, that they may be one, even as We are. ·

. . . that they may all be one; even as Thou, Father, art in Me, and I in Thee, that they also may be in Us; that the world may believe that Thou didst send Me.

(John 17:3, 11, 21)

16

If we would have this closeness to Christ, we must leave everything and cling to the one great love of our life, our First Love. Jesus never apologized for these requirements since they are an absolute necessity for this marriage. Nor did He offer any other alternative in case we desired a lesser relationship. With Christ, as with every other person who truly loves, it was *all or nothing at all.*

Amazingly, people did respond to Jesus much as Abram responded to the Lord. Speaking for the disciples in Mark 10:28, Peter said, "We have left everything and followed You." Matthew was at work collecting taxes when he dropped everything to follow Jesus. Simon, Andrew, James, and John were fishing and mending their nets when they left family and livelihood for Christ. In many cases, these people had never met Jesus previously. How could they just abandon their former life at a moment's notice? Again, revelation seems to be the only possible answer. In that moment, they really knew Jesus, and to cling to anything less than Him would have been utter foolishness!

The only rational reason to leave things of such value—family, country, and livelihood—is to have found something of greater value to pursue. We don't leave something for nothing or for something less than what we have. Thus, the major emphasis of the covenant is not what is being left behind, but what we're going toward or gaining. We're invited "*to* the land which I will show you" (Genesis 12:1). We assume there is a "far, far better place than we have ever been," and the one extending the invitation can take us there. Without this assumption no one would ever marry.

Who could sensibly leave family, friends, and familiar surroundings to live a life of misery and pain with someone else? We leave believing we will live "happily ever after." We leave believing we have finally found that for which we've been searching. *The Amplified Bible* even inserts an assuring

17

word along these lines: "Go, *for your own advantage*" (Genesis 12:1), indicating that we will be better off after making the choice to go. Of course, to be convinced of this fact requires great faith, especially when moving from the known to the unknown, as the phrase "the land I will show you" suggests. Such a decision requires such absolute faith in the person making the offer that nothing more is needed than their word.

The Good Life

Knowing our need for the promise of a better life if we go with Him, the Lord gives us a whole series of "I will's" describing the blessings that will pursue us if we walk with Him:

> And I will make you a great nation, And I will bless you, And make your name great; And so you shall be a blessing;
> And I will bless those who bless you, And the one who curses you I will curse. And in you all the families of the earth shall be blessed.
> (Genesis 12:2-3)

While our own ability to carry out the best of intentions may be limited, the Lord's is not; and when He says, "I will bless you," nothing in all creation can keep Him from doing so. We can believe Him absolutely. To illustrate all the Lord wants to do for Abram and for us, the Lord tells Abram:

> Now lift up your eyes and look from the place where you are, northward and southward and eastward and westward;

for all the land which you see, I will give it to
you and to your descendants forever.
(Genesis 13:14-15)

There is no limit to what the Lord wants to do for His
Bride. He as much as tells us, "If you can see it, it's yours!"
Romans 8:32 states very clearly that when the Father gave us
the Son, He also with Him freely gave us "all things."
Everything is included in Christ. Whatever belongs to Father
belongs to Christ as well, and as His Bride we are "fellow heirs"
with Him (see Romans 8:17).

Having such limitless resources, the Lord could never
let His Bride remain in want. All of our needs are supplied
"in Christ Jesus" (see Philippians 4:19). The only thing that
can keep us from receiving what we need is our failure to
ask. For this reason the Lord tells those joined to Him by
faith, "Ask, and you will receive, that your joy may be made
full" (John 16:24). What husband having the means to supply
his wife with the finest fashions would want her to wear rags?
For her to do so would be an absolute disgrace to him. We do
not honor our Lord by neglecting to receive from Him the
very things that would bring glory and honor to His Name. I
am not referring to merely physical clothing, for that would
satisfy our own vanity, but rather the greater gifts we are to
be clothed with—wisdom, gentleness, healing, faith, patience,
and other blessings that are obviously a gift from His hand.

The Lord, Our Protector

Knowing His Bride's need for security, the Lord not only
gives assurances that all her needs will be supplied, but also
that she will have His constant protection. The words of the
covenant include: "I will bless those who bless you, And the
one who curses you I will curse" (Genesis 12:3). "The one

who curses you" simply means "the one who wishes you harm." The Lord takes His stand with us against such a person. How could He be a husband and not do so? If someone wishes to harm his wife, the husband's place is between the beloved and her assailant where he can defend her. There we find our Lord comforting us with the words, "In order to get to you, they've got to get by Me; and this they cannot do!"

The Lord, Our Shield

The Lord conveys the same idea in Genesis 15:1 when He says, "I am a shield to you." A shield is an instrument of protection against anything an enemy would hurl. As long as the combatants stay behind the shield, they are safe. Herein lies the secret of victorious living. The Lord, our Husband, our Shield, is absolutely impenetrable. Nothing can get past Him to hurt His Bride. But we must stay behind the Shield.

The wife doesn't need to defend herself as long as her husband, who is stronger than her enemy, is there to protect her. She simply needs to trust in her protector. John describes this function of Jesus our Husband:

> . . . greater is He who is in you than he who is in the world.
>
> (1 John 4:4)

> . . . this is the victory that has overcome the world—our faith.
>
> (1 John 5:4)

Resting in the ability of our Lord to defend us, we are perfectly secure.

The Lord, Our High Priest

With the offer of covenant the Lord also promises to take care of us spiritually by becoming our priest. Melchizedek appears in Genesis 14:18-20 to serve as priest to Abram. The Apostle Paul tells us that Melchizedek was actually Jesus introducing a priesthood without beginning or end, "Without father, without mother, without genealogy, having neither beginning of days nor end of life, but made like the Son of God, he abides a priest perpetually" (Hebrews 7:3).

This encounter becomes increasingly significant when we realize the husband was always the priest in a Jewish household. In coming to us as our Priest, the Lord is still approaching us as our Husband. The Husband-Priest is there to bless his family in the name of the Lord. As Melchizedek met Abram, the Scripture says, "And He blessed him and said, 'Blessed be Abram of God Most High'" (Genesis 14:19). When the husband is serving his family properly as priest, the entire family is blessed. Neglecting this important responsibility is worse than letting them starve to death physically. Failing to nourish spiritually is feeding only the body—the temporal—while starving the spirit—the eternal.

The Lord, Our Intercessor

As the priest of the family, the husband not only blesses his beloved in the name of the Lord, but also intercedes on her behalf. Here he is not so much representing God's forgiving love to his family as representing his family before God. Describing Jesus, our Husband-Priest, Hebrews 7:25 says, "He always lives to make intercession." Prayer is the ongoing function of a priest. The husband who doesn't pray for his family regularly is leaving them open to all kinds of attacks from the evil one and failing to obtain countless

21

blessings for them. Christ, of course, could never be accused of neglecting this duty of a husband. There is not a single moment, day or night, when He is not praying for His Bride. He always has Father's ear. When we pray, Father listens, because His Son is interceding for us.

Bringing Up Baby

When the covenant is repeated in Genesis 15:1, 5-6, the Lord tells Abram to try and count the stars, and then adds, "So shall your descendants be." Most brides want children eventually. The Lord wants lots and lots of children. After his account of the Lord's passion, Isaiah adds, "He will see His offspring . . . He will see and be satisfied" (Isaiah 53:10-11). Jesus tells us the reason for His dying and being buried as a seed was so that His seed would be multiplied (see John 12:24). The Bride is to bear Him those children. We see the first real bringing forth of children on the Day of Pentecost when about three thousand people were born into the kingdom. The Church has been birthing children ever since as an indication of the blessing of God.

Abram's response to the Lord's promise of innumerable descendants is quoted by Paul as the basis for being right with God under the New Covenant. The Scripture says, "Then he believed in the LORD, and He reckoned it to him as righteousness" (Genesis 15:6; see also Galatians 3:6). The specific promise Abram believed was the promise of many children. Do we believe the Lord can cause us who may have been barren all our lives to suddenly bear "fruit that remains" for Him (see John 15:16)? That this is His will is beyond question. The only thing in question is His ability to do the miraculous. Can He indeed make us something we've never been before? Can He make us "fishers of men" (see Matthew 4:19)?

The Ultimate Expression of Faith

A few years ago while reading this passage in Genesis 15:6, I had a special awareness that the promises made to Abram were also made to me, since all believers are sons of Abraham. If the Lord had promised fruitfulness to Abram, He had also promised it to me. I had to decide if I really believed the Lord. As I realized that God cannot lie and His word is true for me, a wonderful peace came over me and an assurance that He would multiply my spiritual children.

It should not be surprising to us that trust puts us in right relationship with the Lord. How can we be right with someone we don't trust? If we approach the Lord saying, "I want to be reconciled to You, but I don't believe what You say, and I certainly don't trust You with my life," we insult Him! A marriage that isn't based on mutual trust is no marriage at all. When we marry, we entrust our partner with our life. We believe they can make our life much richer than we could ever make it on our own. The trust we have in the beginning must continue if our love is to flourish. We must persist in believing our partner to be honest and have our best interests at heart. In other words, we must "live by faith" (see Romans 1:17).

The ultimate expression of that faith is in giving ourselves to another. Thus, we come to the place of sacrifice. The culmination of the Lord's call to Abram and to us is found in Genesis 15, "On that day the Lord made a covenant with Abram" (verse 18). This was a place where the blood flowed and Abram could see life being poured out. The Lord told Abram to take a heifer, a goat, and a ram, and to cut them in two (Genesis 15:9-10). Blood had to be shed in order to make covenant; life had to be given.

In the New Covenant, Paul points out that the blood of bulls and goats could never really reconcile us to God (see

Hebrews 10:4). This bloodletting was simply a foreshadowing of the time when the Son of God would shed His blood and pour out His life on the Cross. This allowed us to be in covenant with Him. But giving one's life can never be one-sided in a marriage—both parties must give their lives to each other. So we see Paul describing those who are one with Christ as having died with Him:

> Or do you not know that all of us who have been baptized into Christ Jesus have been baptized into His death?
> Therefore we have been buried with Him through baptism into death, in order that as Christ was raised from the dead through the glory of the Father, so we too might walk in newness of life.
> For if we have become united with Him in the likeness of His death, certainly we shall be also in the likeness of His resurrection,
> knowing this, that our old self was crucified with Him, that our body of sin might be done away with, that we should no longer be slaves to sin;
> for he who has died is freed from sin.
> Even so consider yourselves to be dead to sin, but alive to God in Christ Jesus.
> (Romans 6:3-7, 11)

The clear meaning of this passage is that baptism signifies we have given up our old life in order to be joined to Christ.

Our Better Half

Abram, as he made a covenant with God, had a very graphic picture of what was taking place. After God told Abram to bring the heifer, the goat, and the ram, the Scripture continues:

> Then he brought all these things to Him and
> cut them in two, and laid each half opposite the
> other.
> (Genesis 15:10)

There, in front of him, Abram could see three examples of two halves making *one whole*. One half by itself was called "husband" to the other half. One half represented Abram, and us; the other represented our Husband who was becoming one with us.

The Ultimate Love

Just before He was to offer Himself as the Lamb of God upon the Cross and the veil of the temple, later referred to as "the veil of His flesh" (see Hebrews 10:20), was torn in two from top to bottom, Jesus prayed for us to have the oneness with Him that only He and Father had known prior to this time (see John 17:21-23). He prayed this prayer knowing full well what this oneness would cost. Afterward, He arose to go to the Garden of Gethsemane, then to trial, and then to His death. Jesus wanted this union with us enough to die for it!

How badly do we want to be joined to Jesus as His Bride? The covenant offer has been made. We have been promised security beyond our wildest dreams and safety from any who would harm us. Our priest has come to bless us and the covenant meal is served. The perfect, permanent sacrifice has been made. Will we embrace the ultimate love in the universe and say the "Yes" of faith? Our Lord only asks that we believe Him, trust Him, and respond to the total giving of Himself to us by giving ourselves to Him.

3
Terms and Benefits

Like many covenant relationships, the covenant offered to Abram in the book of Genesis had two sides. One side was what was expected of Abram if he chose to enter into this relationship, and the other was all the benefits that would subsequently be his. Both sides were essential for the covenant to be established. The modern counterpart is the bride and bridegroom's wedding vows. Once the vows are spoken, each knows what is expected of them and what they may anticipate receiving from their covenant partner. If either cannot truthfully make this verbal commitment, then the couple is not married and the covenant is not in effect.

Expectations

Every person planning to marry deserves to know what is expected of them from their future marriage partner. If the husband is supposed to be the primary provider, help clean house, and care for the children, he needs to know before he decides to live with this person the rest of his life. He should not be made aware of these duties several years later. If the wife is required to have a dozen children, be beautiful all the time, and be supportive of every undertaking of the husband, she too deserves to know what she's getting into before making her commitment.

Count the Cost

Jesus was careful to let His followers know what was involved if they would be in covenant with Him. He warned them to "count the cost" and spelled out what that cost would be. (See Luke 14:26-33.) He didn't want a bride ignorant of what she was doing, one who would later change her mind and "divorce" Him. The Lord, likewise, spells out the conditions for covenant to His future bride, Abraham and his descendants, so there can be no misunderstanding. (See Genesis 17:1, 9, 10-14.)

The Conditions

A common misconception of grace is that there are no conditions to grace. God does all the giving; we do all the taking. Some go so far as to say we don't even have to respond with faith, but will all go to heaven even if we are shaking our fist in the face of a holy God.

Nothing could be further from the truth. The covenant with Abram preceding the giving of the law at Mount Sinai is the common example of a covenant of grace, yet there are conditions. Conditions do not make it any less an act of grace, however. Any time God chooses to be in covenant with man, He is giving us a gracious gift we could never deserve. The covenant is simply the terms that must be met in order that we may receive that gift.

The opening statement concerning the covenant recorded in Genesis is, "Abram was ninety-nine years old" (Genesis 17:1). Abram's extreme age at this point would seem to be an indication of his helplessness. Though he had tried earlier to assist God in seeing the covenant fulfilled and having a son, Abram had just made things worse. Now he had come to the end of his scheming and his ability and was prepared to let God do what He promised. He was in the position of depending on God's grace, the only position from which we can receive anything from God. The idea that Abram had any resources left for having a son was so absurd that Sarah couldn't help laughing out loud (see Genesis 18:12). Any notion that we have some source of life in us is equally ludicrous. We are all dependent on a miraculous gift from the Lord.

Once God had established Abram's powerlessness in carrying out the covenant, He then offered His unlimited power, "I am God Almighty" (Genesis 17:1). God seems to be saying to Abram, "Now that you know you *can't* do it, *I can!*" Grace is a matter of letting God do for us, receiving His unlimited gifts and letting His life flow through us. Now that the foundation of grace has been firmly established, the Lord is prepared to spell out the terms of covenant.

The first requirement upon Abram to be in covenant with the Lord is, "Walk before Me, and be blameless" (Genesis 17:1). *The Amplified Bible* uses the word "perfect" in place of "blameless." Though the Lord seems to be asking the impossible, this is an invitation to a privilege beyond our comprehension. Another way of saying the same thing is,

29

"Live in My presence and be complete." What true believer could not want to live in the presence of the Lord and let Him complete all our inadequacies?

The expression "walk before Me" means "live as if you're in My presence" or "act like I'm around." No marriage partner wants to be completely ignored when they're in the room with their beloved. To be treated like you're not even there is probably the worst way to insult a person. Even an enemy gets a reaction, but the person who gets no attention at all feels they have absolutely no value. Of course, the Lord our Husband is with us all the time, and tells us, "Lo (open your eyes), I am with you always" (Matthew 28:20). How insulting it is when we ignore Him all day long, acting like He's not even there. He really does want us to walk through the day with Him, to talk with Him constantly. (See 1 Thessalonians 5:17.) We should not limit our conversation to a worship service or quiet time.

Living in the presence of the Lord brings about our perfection or completeness. He *is* our completeness in the way that every spouse is the completeness of the person to whom they are married, only much more so. Everything that is missing in us is found in Him—righteousness, wisdom, peace, faith, and self-sacrificing love. Whatever we need, He is. Our failures and frustrations in life are the price we pay for acting like He isn't there! In contrast with our continual exasperation and disappointment, we can have a wonderful awareness that Christ is all we could ever want or need. Having Him, we have all (see 1 Corinthians 3:22).

The next condition for covenant is "Keep My covenant" (Genesis 17:9). This requirement might appear too obvious to mention if not for all the people not keeping the marriage covenant—throwing it away as something worthless. We keep what's valuable to us and neglect or abandon what is not.

The covenant relationship we have with the Lord is the most precious thing in our possession. It is to be kept and preserved with the utmost care. We are warned repeatedly not to neglect certain aspects of our walk with the Lord, such as "assembling together" and showing "hospitality to strangers" (see Hebrews 10:25; 13:2). Most relationships that fall apart do so, not through deliberate intention, but the lack of it. Over a period of time we don't give our partner the attention they need and deserve, and then one day, they're gone. Making the covenant initially is a fairly easy thing to do; keeping it is another matter.

The Sign of the Covenant

The final prerequisite mentioned in this passage is also called "the sign of the covenant" (Genesis 17:11). Here Abram is told, "You shall be circumcised in the flesh . . ." (Genesis 17:11). In order to be in covenant with God, the flesh had to be "cut away." Much is said in the Scriptures concerning "the flesh" and how it stands in opposition to the things of "the Spirit." (See Romans 8:3-9.) Doing what we want to do instead of seeking the will of the Lord or depending on our human resources instead of the unlimited power of God is walking "according to the flesh." (See Romans 8:6-8; John 1:13.) This aspect of our lives must be removed if we are to walk in fellowship with the Lord.

Two stubbornly independent people doing their own things and refusing to work together cannot stay married for very long, but our self-willed, self-sufficient nature has been dealt with on the Cross by Jesus Christ. We are told in Romans 8:3, "God, sending His own Son . . . as an offering for sin . . . *condemned sin in the flesh.*" When we could not set ourselves free from this nature contrary to God, Christ became flesh and blood—became sin for us—and allowed Father to deal the death blow to sin in the body of His Son once and for all. (See Romans 8:2-3.) Being in covenant with Christ requires a "circumcision of the heart" (Romans 2:29).

The cutting away of the flesh that represented our sin nature was the evidence that Abram and his descendants were in covenant with the Lord. Without that sign, the covenant relationship did not exist (see Genesis 17:14). Likewise, many have tried marriage while holding on to their self-will and independence; but the commitment to marriage involves a willingness to give up the right to selfishness. Without that commitment, love cannot possibly flourish. This is especially true in our marriage to Christ. We enter into this relationship by confessing, "Jesus is Lord" (see Romans 10:9), thus giving ourselves completely to Him. The reason so many "fall away from the faith" is that they have never allowed the Lord to cut away their selfish nature. They have never made the total surrender necessary to be His Bride. If we approach Christianity with the attitude, "I'll try it awhile, but I can always leave by the back door if it doesn't work," it will not work because the commitment is missing. However, those who give themselves completely to Jesus find great fulfillment in it.

The sign of covenant in our society is the wedding ring. The ring symbolizes that we have given up our self-centeredness and our life now involves and revolves around another. Some have imagined the two rings on the hands of the husband and wife as two links in an invisible chain between them saying, "We now belong to each other and no longer belong to ourselves." Whether the outward wedding ring that everyone can see or the inward circumcision of the heart that the Lord alone can see, the meaning is the same—we have entered into covenant.

The Benefits

When we consider the terms of covenant, we realize what we thought was going to be so costly for us is actually to our gain. In this valuable relationship we have the privilege of living in the presence of the Lord. He completes us. He cuts away our selfish heart and gives us one that is capable of loving. There are even more benefits besides. Most of these blessings begin with the words, "I will," indicating a promise from the Lord.

The Mathematics of the Covenant

The first benefit is the promise of multiplication.

> And I will establish My covenant between Me and you, And I will multiply you exceedingly.
> (Genesis 17:2)

In Abram's day, the greatest blessing of all was having lots of children. To see one's life reproduced over and over again to be passed on for generations to come, this was true joy. The only alternative was to see the family line extinguished.

Our Lord desires many children reflecting His image. In fact, His reason for giving us such "precious and magnificent promises" is "*in order that* by them you might become partakers of *the divine nature*" (2 Peter 1:4). He wants to see His life multiplied many times over, filling the whole earth. The very first command given to Adam before he sinned was, "Be fruitful and multiply and fill the earth" (Genesis 1:28). Once Adam lost the image of God through sin, it became impossible to fill the earth with children in the likeness of the Lord. But a new creation was begun with the Second Adam, Jesus.

> The first man, Adam, became a living soul.
> *The last Adam* became a life-giving spirit.
> (1 Corinthians 15:45, emphasis mine)

Whoever has His seed in them reflects His nature.

No one who is born of God practices sin,
because His seed abides in him; and he cannot sin,
because he is born of God.

(1 John 3:9)

The blessing of multiplication is the direct result of being
in union with the Lord. Jesus said, "He who abides in Me,
and I in him, he bears much fruit; for apart from Me you can
do nothing" (John 15:5). Whoever heard of having a baby by
yourself? It is impossible, physically and spiritually. Bearing
fruit—having a baby spiritually—depends entirely on losing
ourselves in oneness with the Lord. Yet too many try to build
the Church without the essential intimacy with the Lord.
Regardless of how many ingenious programs we may devise,
how much money and energy we may spend, the verdict of
the Lord remains intact: "Apart from Me you can do nothing!"

A New Name

At this point in the covenant, Abram's name is changed
to Abraham, signifying a change in nature:

No longer shall your name be called Abram,
But your name shall be Abraham; For I will make
you the father of a multitude of nations.

(Genesis 17:5)

With the cutting away of the flesh, Abram became a
whole new person. A new person needs a new name. This,
too, is typical in a marriage. Before my wife and I were
married, her name was Marsha Metts; but following the

ceremony she became Mrs. Tom Moye. This name change signified a decision to become a whole new person in union with me. Prior to our marriage she had been a carefree artist, but she has become a wife and mother and many other things she would not have been otherwise since making that sacred covenant.

All of us, in a very real way, need a name change and a new nature. The old nature is selfish, independent, and completely inadequate. We must allow the Lord to dispense with it like a carcass in need of burial. (See Romans 6:4.) But what is our new nature like? It must be in the likeness of the Lord Himself. In Romans 13:14 we are instructed, "Put on the Lord Jesus Christ." We can actually put on His nature. However, this can take place only after the old nature has been laid aside.

> ... that, in reference to your former manner of life, you lay aside the old self, which is being corrupted in accordance with the lusts of deceit,
>
> and that you be renewed in the spirit of your mind,
>
> and put on the new self, which in the likeness of God has been created in righteousness and holiness of the truth.
>
> (Ephesians 4:22-24)

This new nature is described for us:

> Do not lie to one another, since you laid aside the old self with its evil practices,
>
> and have put on the new self who is being renewed to a true knowledge according to the image of the One who created him

> And so, as those who have been chosen of God,
> holy and beloved, put on a heart of compassion,
> kindness, humility, gentleness and patience; . . .
> And beyond all these things put on love, which
> is the perfect bond of unity.
>
> (Colossians 3:9-10, 12,14)

Having this change in nature, we, like Saul of Tarsus,
are given a new name as well.

> I will give him a white stone, and a new name
> written on the stone which no one knows but he
> who receives it.
>
> (Revelation 2:17)

The Lord, Our Joy

Once the Lord enabled Abraham (and his descendants)
to become his truest self by changing his name and nature,
He then promises to be Himself to Abraham, "I will . . . be
God to you and to your descendants after you" (Genesis
17:7). Our God is that which we worship and look to as our
source of joy. Here the Lord is promising to be our source
of joy. A husband should surely bring joy to his wife in
every way possible. Our Lord does exactly that for us, His
Bride. In John 15:11, He says, "These things I have spoken
to you, that My joy may be in you, and that your joy may be
made full."

In truth, the Lord Himself is our joy, the delight of our
life. This joy cannot be taken away now that He is risen
because He cannot be taken away. (See John 16:22.) Our joy

is simply the result of our worship and rejoicing in Him. We are told to "Rejoice in the Lord always [all the time]" (Philippians 4:4). This is for our own good, because when we do, we have the joy the Lord intends us to have. Marriage is supposed to be a life of delighting in the one we love. When it is, the home is heaven on earth. Likewise, our walk with the Lord is to be a continual delighting in Him. (See Psalm 37:4.) When it is, we know what it is to be part of the kingdom of heaven. (See Romans 14:17.)

To be our God, the Lord must not only be our source of joy, He must also be in control. God is by definition sovereign and omnipotent—greater than anything else. If there were anything or anyone greater than God, He would no longer be God. Herein is the fallacy of the false god. Money and the economy have a certain amount of power in our lives; friends have their influence; even the sun controls crops and our physical activities to some extent; but nothing else in all the universe has absolute power except the Lord who created the universe. He directs the sun, moon, and stars. He controls the economy and can bless any nation He chooses. He sets up kingdoms and puts down kingdoms and determines the ultimate destiny of men.

Why would we put our trust in anything or anyone less than Him? Who wants a ninety-pound weakling for a husband when you can have the Almighty? We have nothing to fear. The Lord loves us and He really is in control. Nothing in all creation can rob us of the joy He intends us to have. (See John 16:22; Romans 8:31-39.)

The Result

The terms having been offered and accepted and the resulting benefits having been promised, the covenant is now in effect. The result is what the Lord intended all along—true love. In the chapters following Genesis 17, we are given several examples of how this love is expressed.

When the Lord was about to destroy Sodom and Gomorrah, He asked, "Shall I hide from Abraham what I am about to do?" (Genesis 18:17), as if it were unthinkable to not disclose what was on His heart to the one in covenant with Him. Being in covenant means having an open heart. One of the deepest longings of the human heart is to have someone with whom you can share anything and everything and still be loved. Marriage should be the fulfillment of that desire. Secrets and pretense become absurd between couples who have a deep trust and love for one another.

The Lord has a similar desire to share His heart with us. David was a covenant man, "a man after God's own heart" (Acts 13:22). He took the time to listen when the Lord had something to say; he really wanted to know what the Lord had on His heart. Others have known what was on God's heart because they took the time to listen—Noah, Moses, Samuel, Peter, Paul, John, and literally thousands more. Closeness requires good communication, and at least half of that process is listening. We need to be open and honest, and sometimes we need to be quiet.

Another expression of the love that follows covenant is found in the actual fulfillment of the promise. Genesis 21:1 reads, "Then the Lord took note of Sarah *as He had promised*, and the Lord did for Sarah *as He had promised*." Trust is the foundation of love. Being people of integrity and keeping our word is what makes trust possible. How can we love someone we cannot trust? Therefore, the Lord proves Himself trustworthy and deserving of the love Abraham has for Him by keeping His word.

This is also a part of good communication, to *say what we mean and mean what we say*. Broken promises break down relationships. Even promises given with the best of intentions, if we are negligent in carrying out those intentions, can do great harm. That is why the Scriptures are so insistent about the Lord doing *everything* He's promised and the Word of the Lord *always* being fulfilled. If we are to be a Bride that brings honor and glory to the Name of the Lord and makes others want to trust Him the way that we do, we must also be promise keepers. How can the lost believe the Gospel if they can't believe other things we've said? How can they trust the One we represent if they can't trust us?

The ultimate expression of love on the part of Abraham was in the offering of his son, Isaac. Chapter 22 of Genesis begins with the words, "Now it came about after these things that God tested Abraham, and said to him, 'Take now your son, your only son whom you love, Isaac . . . and offer him . . . as a burnt offering'" (Genesis 22:1-2). Love must be tested in order to know if it's *true* love. Couples who have been through a lot of pain together can say, "I know they love me because they went through this for me." That is the proof of their partner's love; their love when tested proved true.

Anything else in the world would have been easier for Abraham to give than to give his "only son." This was his dearest possession, the one thing closest to his heart. But when asked, he did not hesitate. He obeyed out of love for the Lord. Although Isaac was spared at the last minute, Abraham went through all the emotional anguish of sacrificing his son. That was proof enough for the Lord. (See Genesis 22:16-18.) Abraham's love had passed the test.

Beyond the moment of absolute surrender we find the expression of ultimate love. Accepting the very pleasing sacrifice of Abraham, the Lord responds, "In your seed all nations of the earth shall be blessed" (Genesis 22:18). The Lord is promising to give His Son, the perfect sacrifice of love (Galatians 3:16). As dear as Isaac must have been to Abraham, that closeness cannot compare with the eternal oneness that exists between God the Father and the Son. Nothing could have been more painful for the great heart of God than to sacrifice His Son to death on the Cross. Yet He did, out of love for you and me. He proved His love once and for all by giving the most precious gift of all.

4

A Jealous God

When the Lord made covenant with His people at Sinai, He wanted them to know what He was like and said, "I, the LORD your God, am a jealous God," (Exodus 20:5). This same type of language is used again in Exodus 34:14, "The LORD, whose name is Jealous, is a jealous God." In both cases the Lord is making a fundamental statement about Himself. The use of the phrase "I Am" is almost always an indication of a basic characteristic of the Lord, and the names that He gives Himself are insights into His nature. God is jealous the way God is love; in fact, the love He has for us is *jealous* love.

Godly Jealousy

Paul demonstrated this same kind of jealous love for the Church moved by the Spirit of the Lord within. He wrote, "For I am jealous for you with a godly jealousy" (2 Corinthians 11:2). Sharing the heart of the Lord and His love for His Bride, Paul also knew His jealous care. He wanted the very best for those early believers, and, aware of all the dangers from without, he was determined that no harm would come to them through craftiness or deception. He was on watch constantly, jealously guarding those given into his care by the Lord.

The Dwelling Place of the Lord

This jealous care is given to us by the Lord and His servants because we are His. James writes, "He jealously desires the Spirit which He has made to dwell in us" (James 4:5). The Spirit of the Lord is on fire with desire for us. We were created to be His dwelling place. We are His by virtue of the blood of Jesus, bought with a price. He wants us for His own.

Imagine coming home one night only to find strangers had moved into your house. Naturally, you would be outraged and tell them, "Hey! This is my home! What are you doing here?" We are the dwelling place of the Spirit of the Lord, and He doesn't like sharing His house with strangers. He doesn't want the things of the world to come crowding in and taking over His home. That's why we are warned against friendship with the world. (See James 4:4.) When the world moves in, the Lord moves out!

Moving Day

Before giving the Israelites His list of expectations for those who belong to Him or revealing Himself as a jealous God, the Lord gave His basis for claiming these people as His own. "I am the LORD your God, who brought you out of the land of Egypt, out of the house of slavery" (Exodus 20:2). In the exodus from Egypt, the Lord did what was necessary to free the Jews from their former masters; now they were His. They were no more slaves of the Egyptians, but servants of the Living God.

The Lord even helped them move "out of the house." With the transfer from one house to another there is also a change in authority. When my wife still lived at home with her parents, she was under their authority. When she left their home to be my wife, all that changed. This is a part of leaving father and mother to "cleave to" one's spouse.

We see a similar picture in God's call upon the Apostle Paul. The Lord is explaining why He is sending him to the nations,

> I am delivering you from the Jewish people and from the Gentiles, to whom I am sending you,
>
> to open their eyes so that they may turn from darkness to light and from the dominion of Satan to God, in order that they may receive forgiveness of sins and an inheritance among those who have been sanctified by faith in Me.
>
> (Acts 26:17-18)

"Dominion" is another word for "kingdom" or "house." The Lord wants all people to move out of the kingdom or house of Satan and into His house, the Kingdom of Light.

43

Jesus, the great Deliverer, made it possible for us to do just that, and the gospel Paul and the Church were called to proclaim was that we no longer have to live under the authority and power of the evil one.

A Second Exodus

There is a description in The New Testament of a second exodus far greater than the one described in The Old Testament. Concerning the Lord's ascension after His death and resurrection, the Scripture says, "When He ascended on high, He led captive a host of captives," followed by the explanation, "He also had descended into the lower parts of the earth," signifying the domain of Satan (see Ephesians 4:8-9). What Jesus actually did was rob hell of those who once were in Satan's power. There was nothing the evil one could do about it. Those who had died in faith looking for Messiah met their Liberator King face to face and followed Him out of the enemy's stronghold. Knowledge of this fact gives faith to believers to actually invade the gates of hell in the Name of the Lord, confident that these gates cannot withstand the attack of the Church. (See Matthew 16:16-19.)

The reason for coming out of Egypt is to go into the new house, the place of blessing with the Lord. In calling us out of the old life, the Lord is also calling us into a new life, one of holiness and purity. In Joshua 24:19 the words "jealous" and "holy" are used together. "The LORD . . . He is a holy God. He is a jealous God." Holiness is the nature of God. He tells us to be holy *because He is holy.* (See 1 Peter 1:16.) He wants us to be His companion, and only those who are alike can truly share life together. Since we are so vastly different from Him in nature (in fact, almost His exact opposite), then *we* must be changed. This change takes place in the new birth. Jesus makes it quite clear there is no life with Him in the kingdom without this remarkable transformation. (See John 3:3, 5-7.)

A Call to Purity

When the Lord calls us out to belong to Him, He is also calling us to purity. Paul writes by the Spirit, "I am jealous for you . . . I betrothed you to one husband that to Christ I might present you as a pure virgin" (2 Corinthians 11:2). The danger here is being led away from "purity of devotion to Christ" (see 2 Corinthians 11:3). Purity signifies faithfulness, or pure, unmixed love. When we know we are truly His, we also understand we can never belong to another.

The Map

In Exodus 20:7, the Ten Commandments that followed the Lord's reminder that He had brought His people out, are actually directions on how to enter into this life of holiness and purity. They are expressions of belonging. Each one could be preceded by the phrase, "*Because you belong to Me . . .*"

Because you belong to Me . . . "You shall have no other gods before Me" (Exodus 20:3). Again, the Lord is requiring purity from His people and jealously watching over them to see that nothing takes His rightful place of preeminence. We are His people and His alone!

Demonstrating His jealousy for those who belong to Him, the Lord even gives a warning to those who might create an idol or worship something less than Him. He says, "I, the LORD your God, am a jealous God, visiting the iniquity of the fathers on the children, on the third and the fourth generations of those who hate

Me." (Exodus 20:5). "Hate" is a very strong word for not loving the Lord as He deserves, but with the Lord there is no in-between.

Trying to offer the Lord less than our whole heart is like telling someone you've been dating that you just want to be friends. It's like a slap in the face and is perceived as the opposite of love. Jesus used these same extreme opposites when referring to our choice between loving the Lord and serving the idol of money. He said, "He will hate the one and love the other or he will hold to one and despise the other" (Matthew 6:24). The choice is clearly, "Love me or hate me," and hatred of the Lord can never be rewarded.

Because you belong to Me . . . "You shall not take the Name of the Lord your God in vain" (Exodus 20:7). If we truly belong to the Lord, we want to treat His Name as the Name above all others, the Name to be glorified and not disgraced. There are at least two ways to take the Name of the Lord "for nothing." One is to use it as a totally meaningless term as in swearing. Many refer to the Lord in anger or to register amazement or surprise, making His Name a worse than worthless word. Yet we would not refer to anyone we love like a wife or mother, in such despicable ways.

The other way to take His Name "for nothing" is to confess Christ with no intention of living like a Christian. That's like getting married, taking the name of your mate, and then immediately acting like you have made no such commitment. Why take the Name if there is no real sense of belonging and a desire to live for Him?

Because you belong to Me . . . "Remember the sabbath day, to keep it holy" (Exodus 20:8). The Lord wants us to set aside time just for Him. My wife and I like to designate at least one night a week as date night, a time for us to be alone together. With all the pressures of work and family, this is not an easy thing to do; but the results are worth the effort. When we neglect this very important aspect of our lives, our relationship suffers.

In the New Covenant, Paul tells us that every day can be a sabbath to the Lord:

One man regards one day above another, another regards every day alike. Let each man be fully convinced in his own mind.

(Romans 14:5)

"Sabbath" means "rest," and with the command to keep the Sabbath we are reminded that the Lord "rested on the seventh day" (see Exodus 20:11). As we consistently commune with Him, trusting Him in every situation that arises, we enter into the rest that He desires for us. (See Hebrews 4:1.) When Marsha, my wife, and I celebrate date night, we have an unwritten rule not to talk about any kind of business or work. This is our time to relax and just enjoy each other's company.

I know the Lord wants us to come to Him for strength to do the work He's given us to do. He certainly wants us to consult Him about His will for our lives. But most of all, I think He wants us just to love Him and delight in who He is. When we delight in Him, He gives us the desires of our heart; and there is an end of struggling and striving on our own. (See Psalm 37:4, 7.)

As the previous commands are pictures of purity in action, the remaining ones are pictures of holiness in action. We act this way because God is the way He is. Since He is holy love, we are loving toward each other. The former things are done because we love the Lord; the latter because we love one another; and all are done because we belong to Him.

Because you belong to Me . . ."honor your father and your mother" (Exodus 20:12). The Lord is a God who honors. The Psalmist is amazed that the Lord would honor man as He does. (See Psalm 8:3-5.) We see Jesus honoring His parents and being subject to them.

Because you belong to Me . . ."You shall not murder" (Exodus 20:13). The Lord is the Giver of life in contrast with the destroyer.

Because you belong to Me . . ."You shall not commit adultery" (Exodus 20:14). The Lord is faithful and could never betray us.

Because you belong to Me . . . "You shall not steal" (Exodus 20:15). The Lord is more interested in giving than taking.

Because you belong to Me . . . "You shall not bear false witness against your neighbor" (Exodus 20:16). The Lord is a God of truth.

Because you belong to Me . . . "You shall not covet your neighbor's house; you shall not covet your neighbor's wife or his male servant or his female servant or his ox or his donkey or anything that belongs to your neighbor" (Exodus 20:17). He even channels our desires so that we want nothing He Himself would not want for us. Again, the Lord is calling us to share His life and to manifest that life in daily actions. When we do this, people will know we really belong to Him.

The jealousy of the Lord is there to insure our purity and holiness. Speaking through His servant, the Lord reveals His nature: "For the LORD your God is a consuming fire, a jealous God" (Deuteronomy 4:24). The writer of Hebrews lets us know His nature hasn't changed under the New Covenant: ". . . for our God is a consuming fire" (Hebrews 12:29). The Lord is shaking everything that can be shaken to remove what is not of God. The "consuming fire" image is a very vivid portrayal of the love on fire that is jealousy. The effects of this love on fire are twofold, one for those who are pure and holy, and one for those who are not.

John the Baptist made a similar statement concerning the coming of Messiah. He said, "He will gather His wheat into the barn, but He will burn up the chaff with unquenchable fire" (Matthew 3:12). In Hebrews and Matthew, the idea is to eliminate anything less than righteousness and "burn up" what isn't love. Peter wrote about the second coming of Christ, "The elements will melt with intense heat," and the only thing left will be righteousness (see 2 Peter 3:12-13). One day after the consuming fire of the Lord has done its work, there will be nothing left but love.

A House Afire

This is good news for the believer. We look forward to a day when evil of every kind will be eradicated for all time, and the cancer that has caused all the suffering and heartache down through the centuries will finally be burned away. In the present there is another benefit of the consuming fire of the Lord. As we choose to join ourselves to Him the fire of the Lord catches us on fire as well. Jesus can't have a Bride that doesn't burn with love for Him, so He gave us a baptism of fire and love.

> He will baptize you with the Holy Spirit and fire.
> (Matthew 3:11)

> The love of God has been poured out within our hearts through the Holy Spirit who was given to us.
> (Romans 5:5)

After Pentecost, the people of the Lord finally reflected the love on fire that is so typical of Him. (See Acts 2:1-4.) Christ has been on fire with love for His Bride-to-be from the earliest beginnings, and now she was returning that same kind of love. This love desires nothing but Him, and is willing to do anything for Him and His glory.

5

Redeemer Kinsman

One of the most beautiful pictures of the love of the Lord for us, His Bride, is found in the Biblical accounts of redemption. Hosea, as a type of Christ, demonstrates this redeeming love in his relationship with Gomer, his wife. After marrying the prophet, Gomer sold herself into harlotry, degrading herself in every way imaginable. But the Lord instructed Hosea to buy her back and reinstate her as his wife. In Hosea 3:2, the prophet writes, "So I bought her for myself . . ." From the very beginning we are told this is really about the love of the Lord for Israel and His desire to buy her back as His Bride. Hosea is merely acting out in the material world what the Lord is feeling in His heart.

To redeem means "to buy back" something presently belonging to another. In the case of Gomer, the first man

Adam, and ourselves, belonging to someone else is the result of a deliberate act on our part. Gomer chose to be a slave because of her own desires for pleasure and wealth. Adam likewise yielded to the tempter and came under his dominion because of either the attractiveness of the tree of knowledge of good and evil or his desire to please his wife when she offered him the fruit. By the Holy Spirit, Paul tells us that if we belong to the evil one, it's because we freely choose to submit to him and sell ourselves into slavery. (See Romans 6:16.)

Redemption

Even though we have sold ourselves to someone unworthy of our loyalty and love in the past, redemption is always a possibility. If, in an emergency, a person pawns a valuable heirloom, it can be bought back or "redeemed" once the price of the pawn ticket is paid. Gomer was bought back after her time of disgrace. So also, you and I can be redeemed even though we have previously been "sold into sin" (Romans 7:14). Christ Himself paid the price of our redemption in His blood—a life for a life—to restore us as His Bride.

One of the earliest accounts of the gospel proclamation in the New Testament is found in a declaration of Zacharias concerning the birth of Christ. "Blessed be the Lord God of Israel, For He has visited us and *accomplished redemption for His people*" (Luke 1:68). The gospel clearly announces our Redeemer has come and He accomplished what He came to do—redeem His people.

Sanctification

A Scripture especially precious to me is 1 Corinthians 1:30. Quite often I thank God in my prayer time for the truth contained in this verse: "But by His doing you are in Christ Jesus, who became to us wisdom from God, and righteousness and sanctification, and redemption." The words "sanctification" and "redemption" are actually two sides of the same coin. Redemption means we *don't* belong to the evil one anymore; sanctification means we *do* belong to the Lord. Both are accomplished by our being joined to the Lord by faith and being "in Christ Jesus." The enemy has no claim upon Jesus; and when we are *in Christ*, he has no claim upon us either. Christ has *become* our redemption *and* our sanctification.

Ruth and Boaz

The entire book of Ruth is a picture of what it means for Christ to be our Redeemer. The book concludes with a marriage between Ruth and Boaz, her kinsman redeemer. The Lord spoke through this beautiful love story to let us know what was in store for us when Christ would come to redeem us. As the book unfolds, we see Ruth moving from being alone, abandoned, and destitute, to being part of a family and provided for. Boaz, the kinsman redeemer, is clearly a foreshadow of Christ, our Redeemer. He is introduced to us early in the book as a man of grace, reminding us that our relationship with the Lord can only be built upon this same foundation. Ruth asks, "Why have I found favor in your sight?" (Ruth 2:10). She is genuinely puzzled when Boaz tells her to glean all she wants from his fields and to drink from his water jars. She knows this is not what she deserves since she is a foreigner. She is amazed by his graciousness.

We too must realize when the Lord comes offering us the kingdom that this is *not* what we deserve. That's why it's called "grace." Romans 3:24 says, "Being justified as a gift by His grace through *the redemption which is in Christ Jesus*" (author's italics). Redemption is based upon the kindness in the heart of the redeemer, not some resident goodness in the person being redeemed. Gomer was a harlot; Ruth was a foreigner. We are completely incapable of justifying ourselves and buying our own freedom. That's why we need a redeemer!

Although we cannot pay the price of our redemption, someone has to pay. Hosea paid fifteen shekels of silver and a homer and a half of barley to buy back his bride, Gomer. (See Hosea 3:2.) Boaz also paid to be Ruth's redeemer. (See Ruth 4:9-10.) The price paid for us to be the Bride of Christ is the greatest price ever paid for anything in the history of the world. We cost the life of God the Son!

> In Him we have redemption through His blood, the forgiveness of our trespasses, according to the riches of His grace.
>
> (Ephesians 1:17)

Jesus literally poured out His life's blood so we could be redeemed. He gave His life that we might be His Bride.

Boaz was able to be redeemer kinsman for Ruth because he was a relative and could legally represent the family in buying back the inheritance lost previously. Naomi, the mother-in-law, was rejoicing when she told Ruth, "The man is a near relative of ours, one who has the right to redeem us" (Ruth 2:20, AMP). According to the law recorded in Leviticus 25:25, one had to be a kinsman in order to be a redeemer The whole point of this law was to restore the property sold earlier to its original owners and keep it in the family. Boaz not only wanted Ruth for his wife, he also wanted their descendants to have their inheritance restored.

Christ, our Husband, has the right to redeem us because He is "one of us."

> . . . He (Jesus) is not ashamed to call them brethren, . . .

Since then the children share in flesh and
blood, He Himself likewise also partook of the
same.
(Hebrews 2:11, 14)

Jesus became a part of the family of man in order to be
our representative. He constantly referred to Himself as the
Son of Man to let us know He was doing what He was doing as
one of us. In order to redeem us, Jesus had to die to sin and be
raised to newness of life *as our representative.* (See Romans
6:6-11.) To be our representative, He had to become a flesh
and blood human being just like us. This is the reason for the
incarnation.

As our Redeemer, the Lord not only wants us for His Bride,
He also wants us to have our inheritance. Jesus speaks of our
receiving that inheritance in Matthew 25:34, "Come, you who
are blessed of My Father, inherit the kingdom prepared for you
from the foundation of the world." Our original ancestor, Adam,
sold what was rightfully ours for nearly nothing, much as Esau
sold his birthright. But as a part of our redemption, Jesus restored
what belonged to us as His Bride, then and now.

Boaz, the redeemer kinsman, not only bought back the
family property and made it possible for the family line to
continue by marrying Ruth, he also caused the Lord to look
upon the family with favor. The book of Ruth begins with
Naomi lamenting the deaths of her husband and two sons,
one of whom was married to Ruth. Naomi was without any
sons, and Ruth was without a husband. Not having either,
neither woman would have any descendants. Consequently,
Naomi was convinced the Lord was against her. Upon her
return to Bethlehem she said to the women of the city, "Call
me Mara (bitter), for the LORD has dealt very bitterly with
me. I went out full, but the Lord has brought me back empty
. . . The LORD has witnessed against me and the Almighty

has afflicted me" (Ruth 1:20-21). Naomi believed her family to be under God's curse.

How different is the statement of the women to Naomi at the end of the book: "Blessed is the LORD who has not left you without a redeemer" (Ruth 4:14). Ruth had a son who was the grandfather of King David. Clearly Naomi and Ruth had moved from being under a curse to being in the place of blessing, and Boaz was the means by which this transition was made. Boaz pronounced a blessing upon Ruth, "May you be blessed of the LORD, my daughter!" (Ruth 3:10), *and she was blessed!*

Under God's Curse

Naomi's fear of being under God's curse was not completely without foundation. The Scriptures teach that *we are all under God's curse prior to redemption.* (See Deuteronomy 28:15-68.) Failure to keep the law brings with it certain terrible consequences. Since we have all come up short of God's standard (see Isaiah 53:6; Romans 3:10-18, 23), when the worst thing possible happens, we're merely getting what we deserve (see Romans 6:23).

Thankfully, because of His great mercy toward us, the Lord doesn't want us to receive our due. He wants to move us out from under the curse into the place of blessing. Describing our Husband-Redeemer, the Scripture says, "Christ *has redeemed us* from the curse of the law" (Galatians 3:13, author's italics). Being under the curse meant being in the place of disfavor with Father. But Jesus, like any good Bridegroom, wanted His Bride to be in Father's favor, so He did what was necessary to put us in the place of blessing.

God Is for Us

The move from being cursed to being blessed means that God is no longer "against us" but "for us." In the beginning, Naomi was convinced that God was against her. No wonder she was so bitter. Who can possibly win in life when God is against you? But, in the end, she found that the Lord was on her side.

Sometimes when a young man is dating the daughter of a very protective father, the father really doesn't like the person who is trying to steal his daughter's affection. However, if the daughter knows this is the one person in the world for her and they marry, the father may change his mind and be very supportive of his new son-in-law. He may move from a position of being against the young man to being for him because he married the daughter.

Our position of favor with Father is the direct result of being joined to Jesus as His Bride. We were not in the place of blessing prior to our becoming one with Him, but now we are just as convinced that God is for us as we were previously convinced He was against us. We couldn't possibly win before, but now we can't possibly lose. We want to cry out with the Apostle Paul, "If God is *for us*, who is against us?" (Romans 8:31, author's italics). Boaz, who is a type of the Lord our Husband, further extended his grace to Ruth, "Do not fear. I will do for you whatever you ask" (Ruth 3:11). He not only blessed with his words but was also prepared to demonstrate his love for her by doing anything he could to see that she was blessed. That his love for her at this point is unlimited is undeniable. He has given Ruth a blank check; he has already said "Yes" to anything she may require!

The Suffering Servant

As amazing as it may seem, Jesus comes to us as the Suffering Servant depicted in Isaiah and says, "Ask whatever you wish, and it shall be done for you" (John 15:7). His love for us is unlimited. He laid down His life as our Redeemer, and He surely will not withhold any of the lesser things that will give us joy. This promise is preceded with the words, "*If you abide in Me . . .*" meaning this applies only to His Bride, those who have been joined to Him inseparably. He knows He can trust us with the privilege of asking because, in Him, we no longer act out of selfishness but out of love.

Why was Boaz so kind to Ruth and willing to give her anything she asked? We have seen that his motivation was grace, but perhaps there was something more involved. Ruth must have been very attractive to Boaz, based on his reaction the first time he saw her. Before even meeting her he asked, "Whose young woman is this?" (Ruth 2:5). He wanted to know not only her name but if she belonged to anybody. Then he asked her not to leave his fields but to help herself to all the grain and water she wanted (see Ruth 2:8-9). I seriously doubt that Boaz made this offer to every stranger passing through, but he wanted Ruth to stick around.

Maybe Boaz was looking for a wife. We do know he was wealthy, advanced in years, and unmarried. When Ruth lay at his feet on the threshing floor, he thanked her for not going after young men (see Ruth 3:10). Regardless of how the love of Boaz for Ruth developed, in the end they became man and wife. In Ruth 4:10, Boaz declares to the elders and people gathered there, " I have acquired Ruth . . . to be my wife."

Have you ever wondered why the Lord has been so gracious to us, why He partook of flesh and blood, why He brought us into the place of blessing and offered us unlimited favor? The Scriptures answer with these words, "Do you think lightly of the riches of His kindness . . . not knowing the kindness of God leads you to repentance?" (Romans 2:4). He wants us to have a change of heart and mind toward Him. He wants us to be His bride.

The Lord has desired a bride since before the beginning of time. Little wonder Jesus wants to celebrate now that He has come as the Bridegroom (see Matthew 9:14-15). The Lord has come as our Redeemer, and the reason for that redemption is matrimony. When we think of redemption merely in legal terms, such as being saved from torment, and go on our merry way, forgiven but forgetting the One who saved us, we're missing the main point of what He's done. The result of redemption is to be in a love relationship with the Lord. Anything less is not full redemption.

There are many words used to describe the intimacy that is the result of real redemption—communion, fellowship, a daily walk—but all of them describe eternal life as well. Jesus has told us that eternal life is *knowing Him* (see John 17:3), a term used in the Scriptures to denote intimate relations between a man and wife when children are conceived. The result of redemption is not only love but a new life as well.

After Ruth and Boaz were married, they had a son who was the physical ancestor of David and his descendant, Jesus. Upon the birth of Obed, the son of Boaz and Ruth, the women of the city began to praise the Lord saying, "Blessed is the LORD who has not left you without a redeemer . . . May he also be to you a restorer of life" (Ruth 4:14-15). They saw, in this little baby, redemption from death and the restoration of life. Prior to the birth of this child, the family of Ruth and Naomi had faced extinction. There were no children to carry on the family line. All that changed with the birth of this son, Obed. In him was the extension of life through each succeeding generation. Everyone saw in him and his descendants life going on and on, perhaps their closest concept to eternal life, and redemption from certain death. This was the direct result of the union of Boaz and Ruth.

Salvation or redemption is always salvation from death. Apart from Christ every one of us faces death and the end of our family, the family of the first Adam, forever. (See 1 Corinthians 15:22; Romans 5:12.) We simply have no life in us to pass on until we are in union with the One who said, "*I am the life*" (John 14:6, author's italics). But once we are joined to Him, we have life that cannot be extinguished. The life of God the Son is greater than death, and we have this life—His life—in us. The Holy Spirit spoke through John, "He who has the Son has the life; he who does not have the Son of God does not have the life" (1 John 5:12). The only way to be redeemed from death is to become the Bride of Christ. Once this choice has been made, then we also have the capacity to bear spiritual children, and a whole new creation has begun. (See 1 Timothy 1:2; 2 Corinthians 5:17.)

Boaz, the kinsman redeemer, has been shown to be a type of Christ in offering grace, paying the price of redemption, being a member of the family, moving his bride out from under a curse, being willing to do whatever was asked, desiring marriage, and delivering his beloved from death. Ruth, who became his bride and experienced redemption because of him, is a type of the believer. Boaz was a remarkable person, but so was Ruth. Without certain characteristics that Ruth possessed, redemption would not have happened. There must always be a willing recipient of grace, and Ruth shows us the proper response to the offer of redemption.

Ruth was, first of all, a person of faith. Boaz described her as such in Ruth 2:12, "May . . . your wages be full from the Lord, the God of Israel, under whose wings you have come to seek refuge." She had faith to seek refuge under the wings of the Lord, like a baby chick running to its mother, knowing that whatever the problem, life is a matter of staying near to her.

Becoming a believer and the Bride of Christ is a matter of running to Christ for refuge, knowing that only through a close personal relationship with Him can we have life. This is what we call "saving faith." If the Lord had not responded to Ruth's belief in Him, she would have died. Likewise, we know if the Lord doesn't deliver us from evil, we too will perish. This all or nothing faith that relies on Christ alone for our salvation and redemption is the very thing our Lord wants. He tells us in John 14:1, "You believe in God, believe also in Me." Real faith, the kind of absolute trust that only God deserves, is what our Lord desires.

One of the greatest personal needs of a husband is for his wife to believe in him. To a very great extent, the husband gets his self-image from his wife. When she believes in him, his confidence soars; and he achieves far greater goals than he would otherwise. The Lord doesn't need any help with His self-image, but He does want us to believe in Him; and when we do, we see more wonderful works than if we had not believed.

As an expression of her faith in Naomi, Ruth showed a willingness to act upon the word of her mother-in-law. After Naomi had given her instructions about how to approach Boaz, she responded, "All that you say I will do" (Ruth 3:5).

True faith is the willingness to act upon the word of another. If someone we really believe in is giving us good advice, we will act upon it, proving we trust them by our actions. Abram proved his faith, once the Lord had spoken, by leaving his home and family and going to the land the Lord would show him. Noah proved his faith by *actually building* an ark after he had heard from the Lord. If we truly believe in our heart of hearts, our conviction will show up in our lives.

It is quite clear that Jesus expected this type of faith from His Bride. He told His disciples, "If you love Me, *you will keep My commandments*" (John 14:15, author's italics). He knew that fully committed love comes from absolute trust, and absolute trust results in total obedience. Of course, Christ is the only person we can trust completely without any possibility of disappointment. He has already proven His limitless love for us by laying down His life. He knows us inside out and is aware of needs we don't even recognize. He never makes a mistake. Consequently, His word to us is always for our good—in fact, it's life to us! That's why we respond without hesitation whenever He speaks to us.

Perhaps Ruth's greatest expression of faith in Boaz is found in her request, "I am your servant Ruth, . . . "Spread the corner of your garment over me, since you are a kinsman-redeemer." (Ruth 3:9, NIV). As part of a Jewish wedding, the bridegroom literally throws the skirt of his robe over the head of his bride, symbolizing the fact that she is now under his care. Here Ruth is actually asking Boaz to marry her and to place her under his permanent protection. (See Ezekiel 16:8.)

The husband is to cherish and care for his wife as he would care for his own body (see Ephesians 5:28-29), but the bride must choose to be under that protection. That's where faith comes in. When we come to the Lord, we ask Him to spread His covering over us, to make us His Bride and be our protector, since He is our Redeemer. Then we are not only redeemed by the blood of the Lamb, we are also covered by the blood. Several times in Scripture we read instances of being covered or protected by the blood. When the angel of death passed through Egypt prior to the Exodus, the Israelites were told to place the blood of an unblemished lamb on the doorposts for their protection, and were given the promise, "When I see the blood, I will pass over you" (Exodus 12:13). Even the ark of the covenant was covered by the blood. Inside the ark was the law that had been broken time and time again, provoking a God of justice to wrath. But above the law, on the mercy seat, was the sprinkled blood of the atonement, the means by which the wrath of God was turned aside.

In the book of the Revelation we are told how the accuser of our brethren was overcome: "And they overcame him because of the blood of the Lamb and because of the word of their testimony" (Revelation 12:11). Our final victory and ultimate protection is found in the same atoning sacrifice of Jesus' blood that bought us as His Bride. When we're under this covering, trusting in the death of Jesus on the Cross to pay the penalty for our sins, believing that His blood indeed "cleanses us from all sin" (see 1 John 1:7), we are protected from the condemnation of the accuser, the wrath of God, and from death itself, having the promise of eternal life. We are joined with the Source of Life—He has spread His covering over us—we are redeemed!

6

Love Songs

The Song of Solomon is quite evidently a song about love. Most people would agree that love songs are the best songs ever written. But in order to be the greatest song of all, this particular song would have to be about the greatest love of all time—the love between the Lord and His Bride. There are several levels of interpretation for this book. The first concerns the love of Solomon for one of his many wives; the second has to do with romantic love in general and how the Lord has blessed the union of a man and his wife; and the third deals with the ultimate love of Christ for the Church and our response to that love. Ephesians 5:31-32 says the last two types of love are actually the same. Regardless of how one interprets, the theme of love remains intact.

There are two primary characters in this song. "Beloved" is the woman, the wife, or the Bride of Christ, depending on the level of interpretation. The other character is "Lover" and is either Solomon, the husband, or Christ. As we move through the dialogue and interaction between the two characters, we see love developing through several distinct stages, from initial, choosing love to mature, completed love. I believe these stages describe the growth of a true believer in their love for the Lord.

Stage One

The first stage is choosing love when we realize, "This is the person for me!" Beloved is already infatuated with Lover when she says, "May he kiss me with the kisses of his mouth! For your love is better than wine" (Song of Solomon 1:2). She needs to know she's loved in return, requiring a kiss to prove it. Like a young girl uncertain of her boyfriend's feelings, we also need evidence that we are loved in our coming to the Lord. He has already given us proof that He loves us, by way of the Cross, so we need not feel insecure in our approach to Him.

Beloved already knows the name of Lover, either from firsthand knowledge or reputation, and says, "Your name is like purified oil; therefore the maidens love you" (Song of Solomon 1:3). A person's name in the Scriptures generally signifies the character of that person. Certainly the character of Christ is such that to know Him is to love Him. How can we help but love the One who is Love purified by suffering unto death, our Light and our Salvation, the Lord our Righteousness, the Anointed One?

Since Lover is so wonderful, Beloved wants to spend the rest of her life with Him, "Draw me after you and let us run together" (Song of Solomon 1:4), or, in essence, "Let's run away and get married." The wedding takes place shortly thereafter as indicated by the rest of the verse, "The king has brought me into his chambers."

I can remember realizing shortly after my wife and I began to date, "I want to be with this person all the time. In fact, I can't imagine life without her." Within five months of our first date, we were married. Something very similar happens when we recognize how wonderful the Lord truly is and how we're really not alive apart from Him. We call this recognition and the decision to be one with Him forever, "conversion." The intimacy that follows is far greater than any experienced on a honeymoon, for the union here is not merely flesh to flesh but spirit to Spirit.

After Beloved has come to know the desirability of Lover and has given her heart to him, Lover responds by describing how beautiful Beloved is, "Your cheeks are lovely with ornaments, your neck with strings of beads" (Song of Solomon 1:10). These compliments are unusual in that He says her beauty lies in things that have been placed upon her, such as ornaments and beads.

The truth is, we have no beauty apart from what Christ has given us. We are clothed with His righteousness; that's our ornament and the only reason we're beautiful. How much better this is than being clothed with "filthy rags" (Isaiah 64:6).

The book of the Revelation goes into great detail about all the ornaments our Lord has placed upon us to make us beautiful. After one of the seven angels has said, "Come here, I shall show you the Bride, the Wife of the Lamb" (Revelation 21:9), we read, "having the glory of God . . . Her brilliance was like a very costly stone" (Revelation 21:11). In addition to pure gold, the stones that are part of our makeup include jasper, sapphire, chalcedony, emerald, sardonyx, sardius, chrysolite, beryl, topaz, chrysoprase, jacinth, and amethyst (see Revelation 21:19-20).

What is the meaning of all of this? Our Lord is saying to us, "I have given you a value beyond your imagination in placing My glory upon you. I have indeed crowned you with glory and honor as was My intention in the beginning. Though you had no original beauty of your own, I chose to make you glorious so you could become My Bride."

Beloved is completely conquered by such love and says, "He has brought me to His banquet hall, and His banner over me is love" (Song of Solomon 2:4). Placing one's banner or flag over a fort or summit means that area has been won in battle and now belongs to the victor. Nothing is more certain of victory than the love of Christ—it is the strongest force in the universe (see Romans 8:35-39), and it has completely conquered our hearts as well. We have surrendered to His love and the result is a joyous celebration in His banquet hall. This is the joy of rejoicing in each other, delighting in the One who is everything our heart desires. This is the joy of communion, fellowship, feasting with the Fairest of Ten Thousand.

Stage Two

The choice has been made and Beloved has come to know the joy of her salvation. Now we move into the second stage of love that is typical of the life of a new believer. We could call this phase "asking and receiving love." It is at this point we discover our limitless riches in Christ Jesus. This is a time of great faith and expectancy, of saying, "Listen! My Beloved! Behold, He is coming!" (Song of Solomon 2:8). When we attend church, we really expect Jesus to show up! When we pray for healing or finances or some other need, we expect the Lord our Husband to come in answer to our prayers! And, of course, He does.

This is also a time of loving the Word of the Lord. Beloved says, "My beloved responded and said to me . . ."

(Song of Solomon 2:10), and then quotes verbatim what her Lover has said (verses 11-14). This is a lengthy quote, but she has memorized every word that the one she loves so much has spoken.

I have known of several Christians staying up almost all night studying the Scriptures shortly after they were saved. They simply couldn't get enough of the Word of Life that introduced them to Jesus. While canvassing a community in Kentucky, I met a lady who said she didn't have a Bible but wanted one, so I got her one as soon as possible. I was going back through the same area about three months later and discovered the woman had been converted and had read the entire Bible since I had seen her last.

As we study the Word of the Lord, especially the promises, we discover resources beyond our wildest dreams. Russell Conwell in his book, "Acres Of Diamonds," described all the promises contained in the Bible as a field full of diamonds just waiting to be excavated. When Beloved exclaims, "My Beloved is mine and I am His" (Song of Solomon 2:16), she is not only saying that the Lord belongs to her; she is also realizing that everything He has is hers. She is saying, in essence, "If He has wealth, I have wealth; if He has righteousness, I have righteousness; if He has wisdom, I have wisdom; if He has power and glory and victory, these things belong to me because He belongs to me."

Even in the ecstasy of her newfound love, Beloved must hear two words of caution from her Lover. Twice he tells her, "Arise, my darling, my beautiful one, and come along" (Song of Solomon 2:10, 13), which is merely another way of saying, "Follow Me." In all of her asking and receiving, Beloved may have assumed that Lover would follow her. *He never will.* Jesus can never be less than Lord, even when He is our Lover. Here the Lord is pointing to a deeper love that lies ahead when we, His Bride, are thinking much more about what we can do to show Him that we love Him rather than what He can do for us. That doesn't mean He stops doing for us; it means our focus is more on Him and less on ourselves.

The other word of warning Lover gives Beloved is, "Catch the foxes for us, the little foxes that are ruining the vineyards while our vineyards are in blossom" (Song of Solomon 2:15). Love is in full bloom, but little things can spoil that love. Did you ever wonder how people very much in love can fall out of love and seek divorce? Usually this change doesn't happen overnight, but lots of little things build up over a number of years, and, in the end, the love is spoiled.

Missing one day of prayer and Bible study or one worship service with fellow believers seems like such a little thing, but these seemingly innocent occurrences can be the beginning of a drifting away from the Lord. What we need to ask ourselves is, "Am I closer to the Lord or farther away because of this decision?" If our choice is truly His perfect will, we will be closer to Him afterward. We cannot afford to be careless with the love of the Lord. We cannot take it for granted. "Little foxes" are careless, not worrying about whether or not they're knocking off blooms. Love in bloom and the beautiful fruit it can produce is a tragic thing to lose.

Because love must be expressed, Lover continues to pour out his soul to Beloved, "O my love, how beautiful you are! There is no flaw in you!" (Song of Solomon 4:7, AMP). When we think of Christ saying this to us, His Bride, we realize what a truly amazing statement this is. How can He possibly say there is no flaw in us? I see all sorts of flaws in myself every time I fail to live up to my own expectations or wish myself more like someone else. To look in the mirror and not see any flaws at all is very difficult.

And yet we know that Christ can only speak the truth, *therefore He is speaking the truth about His Bride.* As far as the Lord is concerned, we are faultless—and He knows us better than anyone. For this to be true, there must have been such a fundamental change in us that we can hardly grasp it. We must truly be cleansed from sin; that is, anything that would make us unattractive to Him. We must indeed be a whole new order of being, nothing like the creature we used to be (2 Corinthians 5:17).

We've all heard the expression, "Love is blind," but what does it mean? Surely it must mean love is blind to our faults. When we're in love with someone, we don't see what's wrong with them—we only see what's right! Our Lord sees us only with eyes of love and finds the beauty that may be obscure to us. When I realized this fact, I asked the Lord to give me eyes like His, to see only the beauty in myself and others. I believe this is His will for us, and one of the reasons for giving us glimpses of the glorious Church in the Scriptures. He tells us not to judge each other or ourselves so we won't contradict His estimation of us. If the Lord says we're beautiful to Him, *then we're beautiful!*

Stage Three

I wish this next aspect of love wasn't even part of the picture, but it may be the type of love with which we're most familiar—presumptuous love. Children and parents can presume upon and not appreciate one another's love. Husbands and wives can do the same. Worst of all, we can presume upon the love of the Lord if we're not careful.

I was amazed to find the following description of our love relationship with the Lord in Scripture . Lover is standing outside calling to his Beloved, "Open to me . . . my darling, for my head is drenched with dew" (Song of Solomon 5:2). He is obviously wanting to get in, waiting for Beloved to open the door. The situation here is very much like the one in the Revelation where Jesus says, "Behold, I stand at the door and knock; if anyone hears My voice and opens the door, I will come in . . ." (Revelation 3:20). The extraordinary fact about this plea is that *it is made to the Church* (Revelation 3:14). Christ is trying to get into *His* Church!

I went to a meeting the other day where several churches were represented. Early in the meeting, the leader called for testimonies. For about fifteen or twenty minutes people talked about various programs that had gone on in the church, but in all that time no one mentioned the name of Jesus. Although Christ is to be the focal point of all our activities, we can leave Him outside merely by not inviting Him in. We must deliberately seek His face and His will for us, or all our work will lose the joy of having done it out of love for Him.

Lover has been outside all night as evidenced by his head being "drenched with dew" (Song of Solomon 5:2). And what is Beloved's reason for not letting him in? "I have taken off my dress, How can I put it on again?" (Song of Solomon 5:3). In other words, "It's inconvenient right now!"

Christianity never has been a matter of convenience. When Jesus invited people to follow Him, He received all kinds of excuses. One man said he needed to bury his father first, a common way of saying in the east, "Some other time." (See Matthew 8:21.) When a man (Jesus) was inviting people to a banquet (the kingdom), one person couldn't come because he had a new team of oxen, another had married a wife, and a third had bought a field. (See Luke 14:16.) None of these excuses were acceptable. All of those wanting Messiah on their terms, at their convenience, *were left behind!*

Jesus wasn't worried about convenience when He left His home in glory for us, endured humiliation at the hands of sinners for us, and died a cruel death on the Cross for us. What He was concerned about was loving us, and if that meant doing the most inconvenient thing possible, then He would do it!

The other morning, I was running late to my office and, even though I had found a substantial amount of oil on the garage floor beneath my wife's van the day before, I really didn't have time to check it before she drove to work. To get to the dipstick and check the oil in a Nissan van, the steering column has to be adjusted, then the drivers' seat must be lifted to a forty-five degree angle. Nothing about this procedure was convenient. But I did it anyway. Why? Because I love my wife and didn't want her in peril on the highway.

Being devoted to prayer, abiding in the words of Jesus, assembling for worship, showing hospitality, being a witness for Jesus, and a thousand other things involved in being a Christian may not be convenient. But they are ways to show Him that we love Him, that we're not the Bride who is too lazy to get up and put on her robe to let Him inside.

Beloved never could have treated Lover this way if she had not presumed He would always be there, regardless of how she behaved. Imagine her amazement when she found he wasn't. Her surprise is reflected in the words she spoke when she finally opened the door: "I opened to my beloved, but my beloved . . . had gone!" (Song of Solomon 5:6).

Samson must have experienced a shock like this when he realized the Holy Spirit, who had given him strength, had left and he didn't even know it. Through repeated disobedience Samson had grieved the Holy Spirit so that the Holy Spirit left him. (See Judges 16:20.)

Grieving the Holy Spirit—trampling on grace—is a form of presumptuous love. This kind of love does not yield the joy we've known earlier in our walk with the Lord. But Beloved soon learns her lesson and exclaims, "This is my beloved and this is my friend" (Song of Solomon 5:16). A friend is someone with whom we have a reciprocal relationship. To *have* a friend we must *be* a friend. Beloved is acknowledging the fact that, to a very great degree, she is responsible for what happens in her relationship with Lover.

The truth is, we can stay close to the Lord if we want to, but to do so will take some effort. Many drift away. One of the trends in the last days is to fall away from the faith. (See 1 Timothy 4:1.) Paul wrote, "I die daily" (1 Corinthians 15:31), meaning, "Every single day of my life I must choose not to live for myself but to live for the Lord, to give Him first place in my life." If Paul needed to consistently maintain the decision he made when he first believed, so do we.

The fact that I told my bride that I love her when we first married is not enough. I need to tell her every day. I also need to hear the words "I love you" every day myself. Yesterday's love, no matter how wonderful it may have been, is not enough for today. We all need love in the present if it's to be of any real value to us. Faith, or love for the Lord, is always to be in the present. The question is not "Did we once believe?" but "Are we currently living by faith?" The "good old days" when we used to be close to the Lord are no substitute for being close to the Lord today.

Mature Love

Happily, Beloved finally reaches the stage of mature love, but only after growing beyond presumptuous love. One of the characteristics of this fully developed love is expressed by Beloved when she says, "I am my beloved's, and His desire is for me" (Song of Solomon 7:10). This is a shift in emphasis from her earlier statement, "My beloved is mine . . ." (Song of Solomon 2:16). Previously *she* had been the focal point of their union and her primary concern was what *she* was going to receive. Now, Lover has her full attention and she is interested only in giving herself completely to him.

Often, when I ask young couples why they chose one another as marriage partners, they respond with some form of, "Because he/she makes me happy." They like what the other person does for them; they like all the compliments, the gifts, the attention that makes them feel so special. But if the same couple stays married for a number of years, they will find they've grown so attached that they actually live for each other. They do very little without the other person in mind and are always thinking of ways to show their love.

I believe the Lord longs for us to get to the place where our one desire is to show Him that we love Him, where we proclaim, "I'm Yours! Do with me what You will!" Paul must have meant something like this when he called himself a "bond-servant of Christ Jesus" (see Romans 1:1). Jesus showed this kind of love for Father when He said, "I do nothing on My own initiative . . . I always do the things that are pleasing to Him" (John 8:28-29). The only thing Jesus cared about was pleasing Father, and the only thing we are to care about as His Bride is pleasing the Lord, our Husband.

At this point not only does Beloved realize that she completely belongs to Lover. There may also be a note of surprise in her discovering "His desire is for me" (Song of Solomon 7:10). Beloved has gravely disappointed Lover in neglecting to open the door all night long so that he became drenched with dew. She may have asked, "Will he ever care for me again?" Apparently she has found her answer and rejoices in the fact, "He still wants me!"

In your walk with the Lord have you ever wondered "How could He keep on loving me after what I've done?" But the wonderful truth is, *He does*! He still wants us, rags and all. That doesn't mean what we did wasn't wrong. We've hurt Him very deeply. It does mean *His mercy really is everlasting,* and *His love never fails.*

Mature love is love at its best. Having arrived at that love, Beloved begins to describe its glories: "Love is as strong as death," she says (Song of Solomon 8:6); "Many waters cannot quench love" (Song of Solomon 8:7). Through the persistence of her Lover's love, she has found love to be the greatest force in the universe, absolutely unstoppable. She continues, "If a man were to give all the riches of his house for love, it would be utterly despised" (Song of Solomon 8:7). Here she acknowledges love to be beyond value.

What price can we put on love? Many have given their lives for love; men have given up property, prestige, even thrones in the search for love; and when they found the kind of love described here, no one ever complained of a bad bargain. Love is worth everything, and more. Little wonder the man sold everything he had to get the pearl—the pearl of love—the pearl of knowing Jesus and belonging to Him. Jesus Himself gave up everything for love, and, when at last He had His Bride, He was delighted with His purchase (see Isaiah 53:11).

7

A New Covenant

Down through the centuries, the great desire of the Lord was for His Bride. The prophets speaking for Him were often heard expressing His longing, and His, as yet, unrequited love. They foretold a time when love would have its fulfillment. Isaiah and Jeremiah both knew the heart of the Lord and spoke, by the Spirit, of another day, a better day which they did not see in their lifetime. Isaiah not only wrote about the Suffering Servant—all that Jesus would go through to atone for our sins—he also told us about the love that prompted Him to suffer in such a way. Jeremiah depicted for us the broken heart of the Lord resulting from rejection by His own people. Then the prophet gave us hope by declaring, "The New Covenant's coming, and then we'll be one with the Lord!"

The Prophet Isaiah spoke for the Lord, "Your *husband* is your Maker, Whose name is the LORD of hosts; And your Redeemer is the Holy One of Israel" (Isaiah 54:5, author's italics). Here the Lord is naming Himself, telling who He is; and the name He gives Himself is "Husband." He is not content to merely be Maker, for a creator could be distant and uninvolved with the creation. Nor is He satisfied to be the Lord of hosts, having unlimited power and sovereignty, for even a divine dictator might not be benevolent. No, the Lord, who is Love, has to express that love in terms of marriage, union, intimacy. He says, "Even though I am your Creator and have unlimited power in My universe, I still want to be your Husband."

There Is Nothing I Can't Do For You

Having established the fact that He is our Husband, our Redeemer, the Lord goes on to describe what He can do for us *as our husband.* When He says, "Your Husband is your Maker" (Isaiah 54:5), He is saying, "There's nothing I can't do for you as your Husband. I created you. I can surely care for you." When He declares, "Your Redeemer is the Holy One of Israel, Who is called the God of all the earth" (Isaiah 54:5), He is reminding His Bride of all He's done for her in the past, and telling her that all the earth and the material order are His to give in providing for His Bride.

You Shall Not Be Ashamed

In the remainder of this passage the Lord continues to enumerate all the things He can do for us as our Husband. These are things we can expect from Him once we become His Bride. He tells us, "You shall not be ashamed; neither be depressed" (Isaiah 54:4, AMP). In ancient times, shame was associated with a woman who couldn't have children, as if something was wrong with her and a very vital ingredient of womanhood was missing. This chapter begins, "Shout for joy, O barren one . . ." (Isaiah 54:1)—there is hope even for this one covered with shame.

In modern times we don't consider this condition to be shameful, but other things cause many people to have a similar feeling that there is something basically wrong with them, that something essential is missing. Maybe they're not as smart as they would like to be, or as attractive, or as gifted. The Lord is telling everyone who is ashamed of who they are or what they are that being married to Him is an end to all that. There's nothing missing in the person who is joined to Jesus; we are complete in Him. (See Colossians 2:10.) There is no ability lacking. We are one with Him. "I can do all things through Him who strengthens me" (Philippians 4:13).

Can you imagine the Bride of Christ being ashamed? When my wife and I were to be married, I wanted everyone to know it. I would walk up to total strangers and tell them I was going to get married. No doubt, I was grinning from ear to ear when I told them. I simply could not hide or be ashamed of the fact that the perfect mate the Lord had given me, my other half, was going to complete me. When Marsha accepted my proposal of marriage, she honored me and gave me value I had never known. Knowing I would be married to this wonderful person, shame was the farthest thing from my mind. In fact, it would have been ridiculous for such a thought to have come anywhere near me.

If this is true in our natural relationships, how much more must it be true in our being identified with Christ? Who we are is totally changed because of Him. We are made worthy, given the honor of being His Bride, completed in Him.

Completely Accepted in the Beloved

Depression is often associated with rejection and feelings of unworthiness. Everyone wants to be accepted and appreciated. When we're not, a certain sadness may take over our life. But the Lord has said, "You shall not be . . . depressed" (Isaiah 54:4). We are no longer on the outside looking in; nor are we overlooked and unimportant. We, who were excluded, are now "brought near by the blood of Christ" (Ephesians 2:12-13); we are completely accepted *"in the beloved"* (Ephesians 1:6). The Lord acts on our behalf continually, and His heart is always toward us.

When I was single, I often fought a battle with depression. Starting a new church in a town where I knew no one, I felt unwanted, unloved, and very, very lonely. One night, when the loneliness seemed unbearable, I remember thinking, "This is as close to hell as I ever want to be!" But the Lord knew it was not good for me to be alone, and He placed this solitary man in a family. Now I'm no longer unwanted and unloved, and I'm not alone anymore.

Jesus often said, "I am not alone" (John 16:32), and you and I can say the same. The Lord has promised to never leave us or forsake us (see Hebrews 13:5). He said, "Behold [open your eyes], *I am with you always* [all the time]" (Matthew 28:20). Marriage to Jesus is an end to both loneliness and depression.

Security and Certainty

The Lord continues to tell us what He can do for us as our Husband, "But My lovingkindness will not be removed from you, And My covenant of peace will not be shaken," and then names Himself as "The LORD who has compassion on you" (Isaiah 54:10). By referring to His lovingkindness, the Lord is saying He will be continually looking for kindnesses to do for us as expressions of His love.

Thoughtfulness ought to be part of every marriage. When two people are constantly looking for ways to show their love for one another, without being asked, both of them are quite sure they are loved and have a great sense of security. Have you ever wondered why the Lord does so many good things for us and blesses us beyond measure even before we ask? The reason is that being loving is showing kindness, and the Lord wants us to know beyond any doubt that we are loved.

Much of the anxiety of modern marriages concerns the uncertainty that love will last. A popular song of the past asks the question, "Will you still love me tomorrow?" Though every other kind of love in the world may fail, and "though the mountains [those things we thought would never change] may be removed" the Lord reassures us, "My lovingkindness will not be removed from you" (Isaiah 54:10). There is a love that *doesn't fail!* As further assurance, the Lord reminds us that He has made a blood covenant with us, and the Lord *cannot break His covenant.*

These words, of course, give us the security and certainty we need for the future. We can build our lives upon love that *cannot* fail. We can trust our future to someone who's given us His word and *cannot* lie. The result is peace. The Lord calls His covenant with us, "My covenant of peace" (Isaiah 54:10). When we really understand the covenant, we also understand there is no longer anything to worry about. If this were not so, how could our Lord instruct us, "Do not worry about anything" (Philippians 4:6, NRSV)?

The Lord's ability to do kindnesses for us and His resolve to never stop loving us originate in the very character of the Lord Himself. He is "The LORD who has compassion" (Isaiah 54:10). To have compassion is to "feel with" the other person.

Our Husband is "touched with the feeling of our infirmities" (Hebrews 4:15, KJV)—He understands the way we feel. Consequently, He knows exactly what kindness to do to touch our heart. He understands when our performance is poor because He understands our inner motives. He doesn't give up on us.

No Fear

One of our greatest problems today is fear—fear of rejection, fear of not being able to pay the bills, fear of getting caught, or fear of "the enemy," whoever they may be. Jesus said in the last days men's hearts would fail them because of fear. (See Luke 21:26.) We all know that fear can cause heart attacks. Fear may be all around us, but our Lord says to His Bride, "You will not fear" (Isaiah 54:14).

A woman alone may have cause to fear. If someone were to break into her home, she would be far more vulnerable than if her husband were there beside her. But suppose that same woman was married to the world's strongest man, someone like Superman who always defeated his foes and other evildoers. Would she then have any reason to fear?

We have no fictional character from comic books to defend us but rather the One who, quite literally, defeated death and evil once and for all. Knowing this, can we really continue to fear? Instead of thinking about all the terrible things that could happen to us, our attention is on the One who is there to defend us and says, "Terror . . . will not come near you" (Isaiah 54:14).

At this point the Lord gives us a promise that will remove any vestige of fear. He guarantees, "No weapon that is formed against you shall prosper [succeed]" (Isaiah 54:17). We have become invincible—"more than conquerors"—because the Lord not only protects us from without, but also from within.

John tells us, "Greater is He who is *in you* than he who is in the world" (1 John 4:4, author's italics). If the believer had any idea of the power at work in them or the authority given them *in the name of Jesus*, they would never again be afraid. Truly our Lord has given us authority over all the power of the enemy so that nothing by any means shall hurt us. (See Luke 10:19.)

The Bible is full of examples of this truth. Joseph's brothers tried to destroy him, but to no avail. Pharaoh attempted to murder Moses as a baby, but couldn't. Goliath and King Saul wanted David dead, but he survived. Jezebel couldn't kill Elijah. And Shadrach, Meshach, and Abednego came through the fire because the power for them was far greater than the power against them.

Your Children Also

Such are the blessings of marriage to the Lord. We need not be ashamed, depressed, or lonely anymore. We need not worry about whether His love will last or wonder if He'll understand; nor do we need to continue to be afraid. But there is one more blessing that goes with this union: "All your children shall be disciples" (Isaiah 54:13, AMP).

Couples don't have any guarantees about how their children will turn out when they get married. Even with the best of genes, sometimes there are unpleasant surprises. But the Lord cares about what His children become and gives us the best promise He could give—that they will be like Him. A disciple is someone who is like his or her master. We have been promised that all our children will be disciples, that they will be like the Lord.

God's purpose in saving us is so that we would be conformed to the image of His Son. (See Romans 8:29.) This is true not only for us, but for our children, grandchildren, and great-grandchildren. Since this really is God's will, then He can surely bring it to pass. I am thankful that this is true for my two daughters in the natural realm. Both are being changed into the likeness of Christ. But I am also thankful that this is true for my spiritual children, those whom I have had the privilege of leading to Christ. They too are being changed "from glory to glory" (2 Corinthians 3:18).

All these things take place, and many more, when the Lord becomes our Husband and we become His Bride. Isaiah saw a picture of what was to come hundreds of years before it happened. Jeremiah caught a glimpse of the same vision and declared a day would come when there would be a new covenant and a new marriage that worked.

An Everlasting Love

A covenant broken is a covenant invalidated, including the covenant of marriage. For this reason the Lord tells us that unfaithfulness is grounds for divorce. (See Matthew 19:9.) Israel was unfaithful under the Old Covenant, chasing after the false gods of the surrounding nation. Since Israel had broken covenant time and time again in this way, the Lord spoke of another covenant, "a new covenant . . . not like the covenant . . . which they broke, *although I was husband to them*" (Jeremiah 31:31-32). Clearly, the Old Covenant that wasn't working was to be replaced by the New Covenant that would work. The result would be a proper response to the Lord as our Husband.

The reason the Lord doesn't give up entirely on having a bride is because of the type of love He has. He declares this love in Jeremiah 31:3 "I have loved you with an everlasting love." This is love that existed before time and has no limit—past, present, or future. Therefore, it never quits or "fails" (1 Corinthians 13:8).

Knowing the love that would exist between Christ and the Church, our Lord simply could not stop loving. He knew if He waited long enough there would be a people who wouldn't break covenant but would let Him be a Husband to them. His love wouldn't let Him give up on us, we who would be His Bride.

The Lord's love was also able to say, "Therefore, I have drawn you with lovingkindness" (Jeremiah 31:3). "Lovingkindness" is a covenant word that also speaks of mercy. Human love usually ceases because of unforgiveness or a lack of mercy. But the love of the Lord goes on and on because He continues to forgive. This love draws us to Him and makes us want to love Him in return.

When I was looking for a wife, I wanted someone who could love me just the way I was. I've never been perfect nor have I ever claimed to be. I have faults like everyone else, and anyone who loves me must be very merciful in overlooking those faults and forgiving me when I'm wrong. I also try to have mercy as well, since I know it's a necessity for love to survive.

Whether or not we've found that characteristic in an earthly mate, we can be sure that our heavenly Husband knows all about us and loves us the way we are. He didn't wait for us to be perfect so He could love us, but died for us, proving His love, "while we were yet sinners" (Romans 5:8). I'm glad He doesn't leave us wallowing in the pigpen of sin; but I'm also glad He doesn't wait for us to clean ourselves up before He loves us.

Restores the Joy of Living

A truly loving husband will do all he can to support his wife in her endeavor to be all she can be, spiritually, mentally, emotionally, and physically. Therefore, we hear our Lord saying, "I will build you, and you shall be rebuilt" (Jeremiah 31:4). He is promising to build us up so we can become more than we've ever been before.

The Lord our Husband has given us everything we'll ever need to become all we were meant to be. His riches are described as "unsearchable" (Ephesians 3:8), and He's given them all to us. He is always "for us," and has even given us the Holy Spirit to stand alongside us to strengthen, guide, and encourage us.

With this kind of support from our Husband, we have every reason to rejoice in the fact that we're His Bride. We have an awareness that we're in the one *right* place to be, knowing we have His approval and are in the center of His will. He delights in us and we delight in Him. He is the source of all our joy. In rebuilding us, the Lord also restores the joy of living that has been lost. He speaks of that joy through the prophet, "Again you shall take up your tambourines, and go forth to the dances of the merrymakers" (Jeremiah 31:4).

Many people have lost the joy of living. This is evidenced by the number of suicides and other escape mechanisms that people use. They run from life rather than embrace it. For them, their existence is a funeral dirge and they are obsessed with death, their only evident escape.

In contrast to this funeral march we hear a joyous wedding procession complete with tambourines. We see dancers expressing their joy with their physical bodies, unable to contain themselves. These are the merrymakers, the children of Israel being called in love by their Lord, their Husband, their King. And, if we will, we can choose to join them, to leave the cadence of catastrophe and celebrate with all who have been so blessed.

Hundreds of years before Christ would come to join His Bride, the prophet wrote, "For there shall be a day . . ." (Jeremiah 31:6). Quite often, when the Scriptures speak of a day, they refer to the Day of the Lord and the coming of His Kingdom. Truly, this would be a day to end all days and a time of unbridled celebration. This was the hope of Israel anticipating Messiah. Many of the prophesies concerning the Day of the Lord were fulfilled when Christ came in the incarnation, and Jesus announced the arrival of the time spoken of by the prophets. (See Luke 4:18-21.) Clearly, this prophesy in Jeremiah was fulfilled with the arrival of the New Covenant. (See Jeremiah 31:31-34.) We have cause for limitless rejoicing right now.

A reasonable response to what has happened is to "sing aloud with gladness . . . and shout" (Jeremiah 31:7). We have begun a life of wedded bliss as the Bride of Christ and left the old life of sorrow and shame behind. Life in the New Covenant is presented with these words, "The Lord has . . . redeemed . . . from the hand of him who was stronger" (Jeremiah 31:11).

Before I was united to Christ by faith, life was often too big for me, rolling right over me. I was crushed with problems that I was too weak to overcome. Behind all of my defeat and anxiety was one called "the strong man" (Matthew 12:29), and my willpower and intellect were no match for him. Then I heard someone say, "He may be stronger than you, but *he isn't stronger than Me.* I will set you free from the grip of his power so you can live out of love for Me." Paul knew about this freedom when he wrote, "Thanks be to God *who always leads us in triumph in Christ*" (2 Corinthians 2:14, author's italics).

A Garden Flourishing

Instead of the tyranny of the evil one we now have the opposite extreme. Those who would be in the New Covenant are told, "Their life shall be like a watered garden, and they shall never languish again" (Jeremiah 31:12). What a wonderful picture of rest and beauty in place of slavery and ugliness!

I have had the privilege of seeing a person actually burst forth into flower like a beautiful garden as a result of being in covenant with Christ. Previously withered in spirit, wounded emotionally, unable to become the marvelous creation the Lord intended them to be, they were released into a whole new life in Christ Jesus, and the transformation was amazing to behold.

Joel spoke of a similar time of flourishing in the latter days with the coming of the former and latter rains. (See Joel 2:21-32.) Peter spoke by the Holy Spirit and said this prophecy was fulfilled on the Day of Pentecost. (See Acts 2:16.) We are living in the time of God "watering our garden," pouring out His Spirit upon us that we may flourish as never before. Again, we have great cause for rejoicing.

Some people have forgotten how to rejoice because they are not content. Their heavy metal message is, "I can't get no satisfaction!" But the Beloved of the Lord sings a different tune. The Word of the Lord has come to pass, "My people shall be *satisfied with My goodness*" (Jeremiah 31:14, author's italics), and "*I satisfy* the weary ones . . ." (Jeremiah 31:25, author's italics).

Surely those who try everything that comes along must get tired of looking after awhile. The fact that they're still searching indicates they haven't found what they're looking for. To those "weary ones" who are never satisfied, the Lord says, "Come to Me all who are weary and heavy-laden, and I will give you rest" (Matthew 11:28). With the Lord there truly is deep soul satisfaction that cannot be found anywhere else.

The Lord has promised us joy beyond measure as His Bride, something very much like "living happily ever after." This time the promise really does come true. Now He is ready to tell us about the pledge He will make to us as our Husband, a pledge similar to a wedding vow. He says, "This is the covenant which I will make ... after those days ... I will put My law within them ... I will be their God and they shall be My people ... they will all know Me ... for I will forgive their iniquity, and their sin I will remember no more" (Jeremiah 31:33-34).

Four Essential Elements

Four elements are named here that are essential for any marriage to be successful: *living for the other person, a sense of belonging, intimacy,* and *true forgiveness.* In making these vows to us, His Bride, the Lord is providing all the things necessary to make this new marriage work.

1. God says He will write His law on our heart or *make us want to please Him.* Something "on our heart" is something we really want to do, and "His law" is His will for our lives. The thing we want to do more than anything else is to please Him. And how does He bring about this marvelous transformation? By loving us so much that we can't help loving Him in return and wanting to live for Him. The person who hasn't fallen in love with Jesus, *doesn't know Jesus,* and to love Him is to want to do His will. (See John 14:15.)

The Scriptures depict a married person as one who lives to please the person to whom they're married. (See 1 Corinthians 7:33-35.) If we have a husband or wife, we want to make them happy. If we are married to the Lord, we seek His will rather than just doing what we think is best or what we'd rather do. This is a sign that we're truly in covenant with Him.

2. One of the greatest needs we have as human beings is the need to belong. In high school, we felt that "going with" someone was essential in order to have self-worth. Often youth

and young adults will compromise their principles to fit in with the crowd. This is a legitimate need, but there are right ways and harmful ways to try and fulfill it.

The Lord our Husband wants to be the fulfillment of this fundamental desire. He tells us in the New Covenant, "I will be *their* God, and they shall be *My people*" (Jeremiah 31:33, author's italics). In using the words "their" and "my," He is saying He will belong to us and we will belong to Him.

In a marriage, each person belongs to the person to whom they're married. I belong to my wife and am delighted with that reality. In fact, according to 1 Corinthians 7:4, my body belongs to her more than it belongs to me. My personal conviction is that I have no right to refuse her what the Scripture says belongs to her in the first place.

The Lord takes a similar position toward us as His Bride, "No good thing does He withhold from those who walk uprightly" (Psalm 84:11). He tells us, "All things belong to you" (1 Corinthians 3:21-22), and He will not withhold from us that which is already ours.

3. Speaking through the prophet of the New Covenant He would make with us after the Old Covenant has passed away, the Lord said, "They shall all know Me" (Jeremiah 31:34). To "know" here refers to far more than a mere intellectual knowledge that is the result of study; it is a deep personal knowledge that is the result of intimacy.

We don't just know *about* Jesus, *we know Jesus*. We are one with Him. We share His life. No one needs to tell us about Him. We have the common experience of walking with Him every day. When we get together and tell what great things the Lord has done, we all understand what the other person is talking about.

4. The Lord continues to state what He will do for us in the New Covenant, "I will forgive their iniquity, and their sin I

will remember no more" (Jeremiah 31:34). To forgive is to forget, to never bring it up again and act like it never happened. One of the most harmful things we can do in a marriage is to be like the elephant and "never forget." We all make mistakes and those mistakes may end up hurting the one we love. In order to keep love alive, we need to keep forgiving one another and not keep account of wrongs suffered. (1 Corinthians 13:5.)

Every unforgiven hurt is like a brick in the wall between us and the one we love. If we keep adding bricks to the wall, keeping account of every hurt, there will soon be a very large wall between us. Unforgiveness places the bricks there that separate us—forgiveness removes them and allows us to be close once again.

Our Lord did not desire this wall of unforgiven sin between us and Him. He chose to forgive and reconcile us to Himself. He removed the wall of hostility by absorbing the hurt Himself. (See Ephesians 2:13-14.) That forgiveness is always available, so there is now no reason not to be close to Him.

The Lord offers us a New Covenant with all the elements to make the new marriage work. But just how permanent is this arrangement? Here the Lord begins to talk about the fixed order of creation—the sun, moon, and stars—and says the only way we will cease to be His people is "if this fixed order departs" (Jeremiah 31:35-36). Obviously He means by this that the New Covenant will last until the end of time.

The end of time for most of us is our moment of death when we cease to live in this world any longer and move into eternity. For that reason, when we say our wedding vows, we close our statement of commitment with the words, "Till death us do part." We're saying this is an irrevocable vow, a covenant that will not ever be broken. After offering us the covenant, the Lord makes a similar statement to let us know that the relationship established by the covenant is forever and always, never to be broken by Him. We are the eternal Bride of Christ.

8

The Bridegroom Comes

The Old Testament as a whole speaks of a future time when the Lord *will* betroth us to Himself. The New Testament and the Gospels, in particular, are concerned primarily with a present reality, the arrival of the Bridegroom and His Kingdom, wedding feasts, and our Lord's relationship with His Bride. The Old Covenant has become obsolete. (See Hebrews 3:18.) The New Covenant of marriage is now in effect. The prophecies made hundreds of years before are being fulfilled with the coming of Messiah.

Jesus was asked why His disciples didn't fast. His reply was, "The attendants of the Bridegroom cannot mourn as long as the Bridegroom is with them, can they?" (Matthew 9:15). The Bridegroom and His attendants were getting ready for a wedding. The only time a man is referred to as "the bridegroom" or "groom" is right before the wedding. Jesus spoke as if a wedding was about to take place, and the attendants were there to help make preparations for this wonderful event.

Wedding Preparations

The verses following this declaration explain how to prepare for the upcoming wedding. According to Jesus, those participating will need an entirely new garment. We are warned not to try patching up an old garment and thinking this will suffice. Our Lord cautions us, "No one puts a patch of unshrunk [new] cloth on an old garment; for the patch pulls away from the garment, and a worse tear results" (Matthew 9:16).

Everyone participating in a wedding, and especially the bride, wears new clothes, something they've never worn before. I have seen and officiated in many weddings, but I have never yet seen a bride wearing a patched up old dress for this special occasion.

In our preparing to be the Bride of Christ, do we imagine that we can patch up the old life and appear before our Lord in this garment of our own making? This will never do! We need a whole new garment that only the Lord of glory Himself can give us—that is, the clothing of His righteousness. (See Romans 13:14; Ephesians 6:14.) We don't become His Bride by straightening up the old life but by receiving the free gift of righteousness in Him.

Wine was an important part of weddings in Israel and Judea during the incarnation, so much so that to run out of wine during the wedding feast was a tragedy. (See John 2:3.) To hear the Lord talking about preparing to receive new wine at the wedding is not surprising. He said, "Men . . . put new wine into fresh wineskins, and both are preserved" (Matthew 9:17).

Wine is a symbol of joy and celebration, particularly the joy of wedded bliss. In the Scriptures wine is also a picture of the Holy Spirit. The Holy Spirit causes us to fall in love with Jesus in the first place and then enables us to rejoice in Him for the rest of our lives. In this way the Holy Spirit gives us joy. No wonder the spectators outside the upper room on the Day of Pentecost thought the disciples were full of "new wine" (Acts 2:13).

The question is, "Do we have the proper receptacles to receive the new wine when it is poured out?" Jesus warns us against trying to receive it in "old wineskins" saying, "Nor do men put new wine into old wineskins; otherwise the wineskins burst and the wine pours out" (Matthew 9:17).

Some have tried to fit the outpouring of God's Spirit into dead and dried up religious tradition. Inevitably the life of the Spirit of the Lord bursts the lifeless forms that cannot contain it, and the loss is great. What we need is new wineskins; we need to become a whole new order of creation flexible enough to move with the Spirit of God. (See 2 Corinthians 5:17.) Only then will the joy and the life that the Lord intends us to have be preserved.

The Invitation

Jesus made it clear that He came for a wedding, that we should be putting on the proper clothes for that event, and should be expecting to receive the Holy Spirit and joy like we have never known before. Since these things were uppermost in His mind, the Bridegroom was often found speaking about that wedding. In Matthew 22:1-14 He told a parable that begins, "The kingdom of heaven may be compared to a king who gave *a wedding feast* for his son" (author's italics). In this parable He gave us an allegory of what was going on even as He spoke, and then warned of future consequences for those who would not respond.

Jesus, at that very time, was busy sending out disciples, telling them to proclaim the arrival of the Kingdom and to invite those who heard to be part of that Kingdom. (See Luke 10:9.) The king in the parable likewise "sent out his slaves to call those who had been invited to the wedding feast" (Matthew 22:3). Actually the Lord had begun extending the invitation to covenant relationship to the Jews hundreds of years before, as we have seen in other chapters. Now He says, *"It's time to come to the wedding!"*

The response was less than enthusiastic. The Jewish hierarchy was opposed to Jesus almost from the very beginning. They felt their status as religious leaders was being threatened. Although multitudes followed Jesus for a while, most of the people fell away when the miracle bread was gone. Out of the thousands that He healed, fed, and set free from demonic influences, only one hundred and twenty followed His instructions to meet in an upper room before Pentecost.

Those invited to the wedding feast in the parable had a similar reaction: "They were unwilling to come . . . They paid no attention and went their way" (Matthew 22:3, 5). Jesus came to the Jews first, offering to share the kingdom with them as His Bride. Most of them acted like they hadn't heard Him. As a result, the verdict was given: "Those who were invited were not worthy" (Matthew 22:8). Having rejected Messiah, they were declared unworthy of Messiah.

To reject Jesus is to be unworthy to be His Bride. John tells us, "He who does not believe has been judged already because he has not believed in the name of the only begotten Son of God" (John 3:18). The invitation has been extended to us, and the call to "come" has gone forth—to refuse to listen and respond is to bring ourselves into a state of condemnation and rejection by the Lord. We have done the worst thing possible; we have refused to be the Bride of Christ.

Because many of the Jews rejected their Messiah, "This salvation of God has been sent to the Gentiles [nations]" (Acts 28:28). Once the marriage proposal has been ignored or refused, the bridegroom-to-be has no choice but to find another bride. Happily, that new bride the Lord is seeking is the whole world.

Having seen the callous way in which his first call was received, the king in the parable said to his servants, "Go, therefore, to the main highways, and as many as you find there, invite to the wedding feast" (Matthew 22:9). The highways represent the world, anybody who passes by, Jews and Gentiles (non-Jews) alike. We are all invited to the wedding.

The Wedding Garment

This open invitation did away with all racial, sexual, economic, intellectual, and other distinctions so the Lord's Bride could be *one* new person. Then the Lord blew away another boundary that religious people consider sacred. As He continued His parable, He said, "Those slaves went out into the streets, and gathered together all they found, *both evil and good*, and the wedding hall was filled" (Matthew 22:10, authors italics).

Surely we must be *good* to get in and be the Bride of the Lord? But the Lord says, "No," and He's the one who ultimately decides. In fact, those who have found out they *can't* be good, who realize our entrance has nothing to do with being good or bad, are the only ones who can get in. Jesus said, "I have not come to call righteous men but sinners to repentance" (Luke 5:32); and to the chief priests and elders who thought they could be good, He said, "The taxgatherers and harlots will get into the kingdom of God before you" (Matthew 21:31).

What's required for the wedding is something only the Lord can provide for us, and that is "the wedding garment." This is righteousness far beyond any good that we may have done—it's a righteousness we receive from God *through faith in Christ Jesus.* (See Philippians 3:9.) Jesus is the only perfect person who's ever lived. Since God's standard for entrance into His kingdom is *perfection* (Matthew 5:48), we must receive the Lord Jesus with *His* righteousness and perfection in order to have acceptable clothing. This free gift of righteousness in Christ is the wedding garment, and we'd better not try to go to the wedding feast without it.

In the parable Jesus told, "When the king came in to look over the dinner guests, he saw there a man not dressed in wedding clothes" (Matthew 22:11), and the consequences were catastrophic. The king commanded the man to be bound hand and foot and cast into outer darkness where there is weeping and gnashing of teeth (Matthew 22:13). Thinking we can get into the presence of God while bypassing God's perfect provision in His Son and His righteousness is heading for a tragic surprise. The teachings of Buddha, Mohammed, Joseph Smith, Mary Baker Eddy, or some ascended master, cannot suffice. To refuse the wedding garment for "a better idea" of our own design is to be ultimately cast into outer darkness away from the presence of God.

The Wedding Feast

In Luke 12:36, Jesus cautioned disciples, "And be like men who are waiting for their master *when he returns from the wedding feast* . . . " (author's italics). Jesus was going away after His death and resurrection to return at some future date. But where was He going and what would He be doing while He was away? According to Jesus, He was going to the wedding feast. Since He *has* gone away and *has not* returned with the hosts of heaven to permanently eliminate evil, that means the wedding feast is going on right now. I believe Jesus made the statement at the Last Supper, "I will not drink of the fruit of the vine from now on until that day when I drink it new with you in My Father's kingdom" (Matthew 26:29), because He knew the wedding feast was just around the corner. The new wine of the Holy Spirit was about to be poured out on the Day of Pentecost so that Jesus and the disciples could drink it together in a time of great celebration.

Paul also wrote as if we're celebrating with Jesus right now. In Ephesians 2:4-6 we read, "But God . . . made us alive together with Christ . . . and *seated us with Him in the heavenly places*" (author's italics). If Christ is seated at the wedding feast, *so are we.* How could Jesus be enjoying the wedding feast between His ascension and His return the way He said He was *without His Bride?*

The Last Supper was not simply a foreshadowing of the wedding feast about to take place in the heavenlies. Jesus declared it to be the actual covenant meal when He said, "This cup which is poured out for you *is the new covenant* in My blood" (Luke 22:20, author's italics). When the Lord made covenant with Israel at Mount Sinai; Moses, Aaron, Nadab, Abihu, and seventy of the elders ate and drank in the presence of the Lord. (See Exodus 24:1, 9-11.) This covenant meal was an important part of the making of the Old Covenant—to eat bread with someone meant you were in covenant with them.

Since the Old Covenant had been made invalid by Israel's unfaithfulness, there needed to be a New Covenant and a New Covenant meal. Eating this meal together meant, "The covenant is now in effect. *We're married.*" Every time we eat the Lord's Supper we are recognizing that we are the Bride of Christ and are in covenant with Him. Little wonder Jesus said, "I have earnestly desired to eat this Passover with you before I suffer" (Luke 22:15).

The Greek word here translated "desired" (*epethumesa*) is elsewhere translated "lusted," signifying the strong desire that a man has for a woman. Although this in no way implies that Jesus had a physical attraction at this time, it does indicate the Son of Man had been wanting His Bride for a very long time. Since the beginning of time, Jesus had been looking forward to this covenant meal symbolizing our spiritual union with Him.

There had been other Passover meals before, but Jesus said, "I have earnestly desired to eat *this* Passover with you before I suffer" (Luke 22:15, author's italics). Why was this one any different than the others? Because this one was the fulfillment of all the rest. This was "the real thing" that had been rehearsed for centuries when Jesus would fill the empty chair for Messiah and thereby declare that He had come as the Christ to claim His Bride.

The Consummation

When Jesus broke the bread and gave it to them, He spoke these words, "This is My body which is given for you" (Luke 22:19). Marriage is not only giving our mind and our heart to the one we love, it is also giving of our body, since this is the physical manifestation of who we are. Where this expression of love is missing, we say the marriage is not consummated and the union is incomplete.

Jesus was about to give His body to us on the Cross. He didn't just give us His mind or His heart, He gave us His body. Recalling this fact, Paul exhorts us, "Present your *bodies* a living and holy sacrifice" (Romans 12:1, author's italics). Christ gave His body for us, but have we given our body to

Him? Or do we still imagine that our body belongs to us?

To give our body to the Lord is to use that body to please Him and *not to please ourselves*. We use our eyes to look at things He would want us to see, we use our ears to hear things He would want us to hear, and we use our mind to think about things that would be pleasing to Him. Our body belongs to Him, and we use it to bring Him joy.

That the offering of His body refers to His death on the Cross becomes obvious when we hear the rest of His words: "Do this in remembrance of Me" (Luke 22:19). What are we to remember every time we break bread and drink of the fruit of the vine if not His death on the Cross for us? What must we never forget as long as we live but the fact that Jesus gave His body for us so we could be His Bride?

To further emphasize and explain the union that was taking place during that covenant meal Jesus went on to say as He offered the cup, "This cup which is poured out for you is the new covenant in My blood" (Luke 22:20). Jesus was not only giving His body; He was also giving His life. These Jewish disciples must have understood from the Old Testament Scriptures that "the life of the flesh is in the blood" (Leviticus 17:11), and that in pouring out His blood, He was also pouring out His life. In a very short time Jesus was to do what He described at the Last Supper, shed His blood on the Cross, and in so doing, pour out His life for us.

A man and woman, as they speak their wedding vows, are giving their lives to each other. That's why the question is asked, "Do you take this man (or woman) to be your lawfully wedded husband (or wife)?" The question is really, "Will you receive the life they are offering you and take good care of it as a valuable possession?" When we become a Christian, the Lord gives His life to us and we give our life to Him.

But there is a major difference between an ordinary wedding and our becoming the Bride of Jesus. Christ actually pours His life into us and comes to live in us. His life in us is what makes us a Christian (see Romans 8:9), and is our "hope of glory" (Colossians 1:27). That's why Jesus insisted at the Last Supper concerning the cup, "Drink from it, all of you" (Matthew 26:27). He knew we could not belong to Him without receiving His life.

What the covenant meal portrayed Jesus carried out on the Cross. Here His body was offered up, here His blood was shed. At that exact time in history the New Covenant went into effect and we believers became *one with Christ*. Many cataclysmic events took place to emphasize the far-reaching effects of that day. The sun hid its face to let us know the natural order had been disturbed, dead people came forth from their graves to declare a covenant of life had been established, and the veil of the temple was torn from top to bottom to tell us that everything that had separated us from the presence of the Lord was now gone. (See Matthew 27:45, 51-53.)

Paul spoke of our oneness with Christ on the Cross when he wrote, "I have been *crucified with Christ . . .*" (Galatians 2:20, author's italics). The only way anybody could have been crucified with Christ was to be one with Him at that precise moment in time—*and we were*. What happened to Him happened to us. That's why His death paid for our sin. *His death to sin was our death to sin.* (See Romans 6:6-11.) Without Christ's identification with us, making Him one with us *and our sin*, and our identification with Him, uniting us with Him *in redemption*, there's no link between the Cross of Christ and us. If we weren't one with Him on the Cross, then we can't be saved today.

Jesus insisted that His followers embrace the cross since this was the means by which we were joined to Him. He said in Matthew 10:38, "He who does not take his cross and follow after Me is not worthy of Me." In other words, "If you don't willingly accept the cross as the instrument of your salvation and go with me to the place of crucifixion, *you can't have Me as your Lord, husband, or Savior.*"

When they marry, every couple must be willing to give up the old life in order to experience new life together. Neither marriage partner should expect to continue to date other people or to live as they did when they were single. Without this willingness to abandon the old lifestyle, a marriage simply cannot work.

The cross that Jesus would call us to is merely the place where we let go of the old ways to experience newness of life with Him. It's the place where we die to living for ourselves, which is the essence of sin and the opposite of love, and choose to live a life that expresses love for Him. In Romans, Paul explains our co-crucifixion with Christ in these terms, *"Our old self was crucified with Him, . . . For the death that He died, He died to sin."* (Romans 6:6, 10, author's italics). On the Cross, Jesus died to the self that wanted to live, the nature He struggled with in the Garden of Gethsemane, *because He loved us more than He loved His own life.* He said "No" to self and "Yes" to loving us. He knew if we were going to be His Bride, He would have to lay down His life for us. *There was no other way.* Nor is there any other way for us. If we would be His Bride, we must meet Him at the Cross.

Once we have decided to join Him in His death to sin and selfishness, the Lord says that we are one with Him. After His statement about the absolute necessity of embracing the cross with Him, He goes on to say, "He who receives you receives Me" (Matthew 10:40). Obviously, He is speaking as if we are now one person. The way others treat us is the way they treat Jesus since we have been joined inseparably to Him. Two persons have become one in a holy marriage.

9

The Gospel of Love

The Gospel of John could well be called the Gospel of Love. The author referred to himself as "the disciple whom Jesus loved" (John 21:20), because he was so keenly aware of the love of the Lord. He seemed to be particularly sensitive to Jesus as the Bridegroom and gave us insights into our relationship with the Lord that the other Gospels lack. He alone has the outpouring of the heart of the Lord just before His death (see John 14-16); his is the Gospel of John 3:16.

In the very first chapter, John identifies Jesus as the sacrificial Lamb who takes away the sin of the world and makes reconciliation possible. (See John 1:29.) Almost as if he cannot wait, he tells us in advance that this Jesus will lay down His life for us and give us the greatest demonstration of love the world has ever known.

Wine of Rejoicing

In chapter two, John begins talking about a wedding, a favorite subject of Jesus. Here John says that Jesus did His first miracle at a wedding feast, turning water into wine. Of all the events Jesus could have chosen for His first miracle, why do you suppose He chose this one? Could it be because *Jesus came for a wedding*? Could it be that Israel was like people trying to have a wedding feast without "the new wine" and He wanted to give it to them along with joy beyond their imagination?

There didn't seem to be a lot of joy among God's people when Jesus arrived, just a lot of rules and burdens the people couldn't bear. (See Matthew 23:4.) But the Lord has always wanted His people to celebrate and rejoice in His love, so He made it possible for us to receive the new wine of the Holy Spirit and to become God's joyful people.

One of the saddest things that could be said of the Church today is, "They have no wine!" (John 2:3). Where worship services have become a matter of form and ritual with no life, no dancing in the heart, no spirit of true delight in the love of the Lord; where church has become a business institution where finances and maintaining the program are of primary concern, and people are merely statistics, *we need a miracle of the first order*. And this is the very place where Jesus begins to demonstrate His miracle-working power.

A New Home

For couples getting married, a very important part of preparing for the wedding is finding a place to live after they are wed. I'll never forget looking with my future bride for the house where we would begin our life together as husband and wife. The first place that we considered was previously occupied by a photographer, and he had painted the bathroom walls black.

The next place had no windows in the entire house, only sliding glass doors at the front and rear of the house. Finally we decided on an octagonal house with windows all the way around.

Jesus, in looking forward to the upcoming wedding, was concerned with providing a place for His Bride, and so we find Him saying in John 14:2, "I go to prepare a place for you." *Where was He going* in order to provide this place for us? Was He about to ascend into heaven as He spoke with His disciples on this occasion, or *was He about to go to the Cross?* Surely from the context we can see that the thing uppermost on the mind of Jesus at this time was going to the Cross. (See John 13:31; 15:13; 16:16-20.) Here He tells us in advance *the reason for His going to the Cross was to prepare a place for us.*

Jesus continued to explain His purpose for going to the Cross, "And if I go and prepare a place for you, I will come again and receive you to Myself; *that where I am* [present tense, not future], there you may be also" (John 14:3). Did Jesus "come again" to His disciples after His death on the Cross? Clearly He did (see John 20:14-21, 23), and their sorrow was turned into joy by the sight of their resurrected Savior just like He said it would be. (See John 16:20.)

But what is this place He has prepared for us and where may we expect to be now that He has indeed died on the Cross? The key is in the phrase " . . . that *where I am* . . . " (John 14:3). Jesus spoke of a present reality that His Bride would be able to enjoy once He had died on the Cross and become "the Way" (John 14:6). But where was Jesus at that exact moment in time when He was speaking to His disciples about "where I am"? Was He not in Father's presence *right then* as He talked about being the exclusive avenue to Father?

Another way of saying, "in Father's presence" is "in My Father's house" (John 14:2).

Father's house is where Father lives. To be in the Father's house is to be in His presence. Jesus died so we could live in Father's presence the way He had always lived in Father's presence; and we can experience this reality today because Jesus has already died, and His death accomplished what He said it would!

Once Jesus had established the fact that His Cross makes it possible for us to live in Father's presence, He went on to describe what life in Father's presence would be like. Jesus never did just what He wanted to do but did what He saw Father doing. Consequently, when we live in Father's presence, we will do His will as well. Jesus tells us, "He who believes in Me, the works that I do shall he do also; and greater works than these shall he do, because I go to the Father" (John 14:12). As long as Jesus was here in the flesh, Father could accomplish His will through Him. But now that Christ has ascended, Father wants other hands and feet and lips to cooperate in seeing His will done on earth.

Cooperation

Working together is an essential part of a happy home. Before a man and woman decide to get married, they should consider whether or not they have the same goals in life and can assist one another in reaching those goals. They might discuss the type of family they hope to have, financial expectations, and the spiritual environment they consider desirable as they live their lives together. Where there is no agreement on the basic ingredients that make life fulfilling, the couple may spend much of their time working against one another and experience a great deal of frustration.

As the Bride of Christ, we want to be going the same direction He is going, working with Him in the things that please Him most. The greatest desire in the heart of the Lord is to do Father's will. Naturally we will want to do the same. In fact, when we come into covenant relationship by the blood of Jesus, we get a new heart that delights to do His will (see Jeremiah 31:33) *so we can cooperate with Jesus and do the works that He did.*As we freely choose Father's will and "get in the yoke with Jesus" (Matthew 11:28-30), we find that Christ in us is doing all the work and the burden is light indeed.

Assuming a spirit of cooperation, our Lord gives us a magnificent promise to provide anything we need to see Father's will done. He says, "And whatever you ask in My Name, that will I do, *that* the Father may be glorified in the Son. If you ask Me anything in My Name, I will do it" (John 14:13-14). The word "and" links the promise with the fact that we are doing His works and not acting independently. This promise, then, does not apply when we are praying with a selfish motive and not to glorify Father. (See James 4:3.) To pray in Jesus' Name is to pray what Christ Himself would pray, and His motivation was *always* to glorify Father.

When we truly pray in Jesus' name in order to see Father glorified, we have the guarantee of receiving what we need. Christ is right there in Father's presence to ask on our behalf (see Hebrews 7:25), and we are there with Him, having been united with Him by faith. Father hears us when we pray.

Fully Equipped

None of us would ask someone to do a job for us without making sure they had the tools and materials necessary to get the job done. If we wanted a hole dug, we would provide the pick or shovel required to dig it. If we wanted a cake baked, we'd make sure the flour, sugar, eggs, milk, and other ingredients were available. To do any less would be absurd. When the Lord lets us know His will for our lives and the work He would have us do, will He do any less for us? Surely in Father's house we can expect to be supplied with anything that's needed to see His will accomplished.

Communication

In Father's presence there is also a lot of listening. Ego loves to talk; love learns to listen. Jesus said, "If you love me, *you will keep My commandments* (hang on to My words)" (John 14:15, author's italics). We keep what's valuable to us and let go of what is not. If someone's words aren't worth much to us, we soon forget them and certainly do not live by them or act on them. But if they are precious to us *because we love the one who said them*, we will do our best to act accordingly and let them know we were really listening.

I still have love notes from my beloved going back to the early days of our marriage. I keep letters and cards that our girls gave me just because they love me. I will never willingly relinquish these very precious words given me by the ones who mean so much to me. Even when I go to the grocery store, I take a list written in very familiar handwriting so I can be sure and please the one I love. These words are important to me.

If we will just read and listen, the Lord our Husband has words of love for us too precious to throw away. He'll tell us how to please Him, but He will never shout; instead, He will speak to us in a quiet moment with a "still, small voice," a gentle voice that draws us closer to Him. Hearing His voice is easy when you're in Father's house.

Abiding Love

The theme of living in Father's presence today is taken a step further in John 15, a chapter all about "abiding." "Abode" is another word for "house," or the place where a person habitually lives; and "abiding" is living together in the same place, which is the whole purpose of getting married. Dating is fine for a while, but as love continues to grow, the times in between seeing the one we love become unbearable. We want to be with them all the time, so we get married and move into the same house.

Jesus says to us, "Abide in Me, and I in you," (John 15:4), or "Live in Me and let Me live in you." If this is not being in the same place at the same time, I don't know what is. But this goes beyond just being in Father's house together, although we are that. Jesus is talking about *being in each other*, Christ in us and us in Christ, or absolute intimacy. This is the culmination of our marriage to Him and the oneness we have longed for all of our lives.

Once He has invited us into this relationship, there is no compromise, no "just being friends." He tells us, "If anyone *does not* abide in Me, he is thrown away" (John 15:6, author's italics). At this point, there is either total acceptance of one another and unity, or complete rejection. Nothing in between. Most love relationships come to this place where we either go on into the depths of love or we part company. A decision must be made.

If we choose to move into Father's house with Jesus and to go deeper in love with Him, *He will fulfill our heart's desires.* He promises, "If you abide in Me and My words abide in you, *ask whatever you wish, and it shall be done for you*" (John 15:7, author's italics). When we give ourselves without reservation to Him, He gives Himself without reservation to us, and what He has to offer is unlimited!

Abiding Love Produces Fruit

Living in the same house together and enjoying the type of intimacy described here usually results in having children.

And what is the reason the Lord gives us for abiding in Him? "Abide in Me, and I in you. As the branch cannot *bear fruit* of itself unless it abides in the vine, so neither can you, unless you abide in Me . . . he who abides in Me, and I in him, he *bears much fruit*; for apart from Me you can do nothing" (John 15:4-5, author's italics). "Bear fruit" is another way of saying "have children." The Lord is telling us to abide in Him so that we can have children for Him—spiritual children—sons and daughters in the faith.

A woman cannot have a child by herself. She must become one with her husband or she will never have a baby. If we try to build the church and bring converts to the faith without a vital union with the Lord our Husband, we will meet with a stunning lack of success. Jesus tells us this procedure *will not work*. We must make that total surrender of ourselves that allows His life to flow through us if we ever want to "bear fruit" for Him.

Joy

Living in Father's house with Jesus, abiding in Him as He abides in us, letting Him fulfill all our desires, and bearing fruit for Him must surely result in our having joy. By telling us how to live in Father's house, Jesus is really telling us how to have joy. He says, "These things I have spoken to you that My joy may be in you, and that your joy may be made full" (John 15:11). Jesus knows how to have joy, and He wants His Bride to know how to share that joy.

Jesus had joy when others would have given up in despair. The writer of Hebrews states that the joy set before Him was what enabled Him to endure the Cross. (See Hebrews 12:2.) But what was the secret of this full and complete and constant joy—joy that gave Him strength to go through the impossible? Jesus had learned to live the reality described in

Psalm 16:11, "In Thy presence is fulness of joy; in Thy right hand there are pleasures forever." He had been in Father's presence always. Now He was teaching His Bride to dwell in that place of unending joy.

Love

Before expressing His desire for us to have His joy, Jesus tells us His secret of eternal joy, "If you keep My commandments, you will abide in My love; just as I have kept My Father's commandments, and abide in His love" (John 15:10). The way to have perpetual joy is to *stay in love*, and the way to stay in love is to *live to please the one you love*. People fall out of joy when they fall out of love, and they fall out of love when they begin to think more of themselves than they do the one they once loved.

Some of the saddest songs written are about love that has been lost. Some of the saddest people I've known are people who once had the joy of the Lord, but have left their first love. But even if this has happened to us, we can pray with David, known as "a man after God's own heart" (Acts 13:22), "Restore to me the *joy* of Thy salvation" (Psalm 51:12, author's italics). We can choose to begin again living for the One we love and have the joy of knowing we're in His favor.

The Greatest Love

Living in Father's house is having fullness of joy and living a life of love, so Jesus tells us how to live in love. After commanding us to love one another as He has loved us, He says, "Greater love has no one than this, that one lay down His life for His friends" (John 15:13). As we have already seen, Jesus was about to do just that, and He tells us to follow His example. He says, "If you're really serious about loving, you must lay down your life."

True love, then, is putting someone else ahead of ourselves, laying down our life for them. The exact opposite of love is what we hear so much today, "Me first! My rights are all that matter." The result is chaos and violence like we have never known in this country. Self-realization is often a group of people trying to be gods; and in their struggle for preeminence, there is little room for love, marriage, or joy.

Marriage, which is based on love, must be a matter of laying down our life for another. When we say the wedding vows, we are giving our life away. But is that the end? A few years ago my wife and I said our marriage vows again to let each other know we still felt the way we did when we first were married. We still wanted to give our lives to each other on a regular basis.

Paul seemed to think this attitude was important in our relationship with the Lord. He didn't just repeat his wedding vows to the Lord every twenty- or twenty-five years, but wrote, "I die daily" (1 Corinthians 15:31). Jesus also spoke about taking up our cross daily. (See Luke 9:23.) When this commitment to put the other person first is not renewed periodically, a love can grow cold and die.

Honesty and Openness

Along with joy and love, there is also openness and honesty in Father's house with Jesus. He continues to describe our life together by saying, "I have called you friends, for all things that I have heard from My Father, I have made known to you" (John 15:15). True friends are those to whom we can tell anything and everything, and a husband and wife should be the best of friends. Secrets kept may separate, but secrets shared bring us closer together. Jesus wants to share His deepest secrets with us, His Bride.

On the other hand, there is nothing about which we can't talk to Jesus. What we can tell no one else, we can tell Him. Whatever we may say, He already knows and is probably waiting for us to discover. We can live in complete openness with Him. John was referring to this fact when he wrote, "If we walk in the light [out in the open, unashamed] as He Himself is in the light [He has been open with us], we have fellowship with one another" (1 John 1:7). Our not hiding any secrets from each other is what enables us to be close, and knowing He will love us no matter what we may confess (see 1 John 1:9) is what makes it possible for us to be so honest with Him.

A New Name

Life in Father's house with Jesus is wonderful, but before we can enjoy any of this bliss, one thing must happen. We must take the name of Christ. When a man and woman are married, the wife usually takes the name of her husband. When my wife and I were married, she became Mrs. Tom Moye. Here Jesus says, "All these things they will do to you *for My name's sake*" (John 15:21), or "because you have *My name*."

Taking the name signifies becoming a new person. We're no longer the person we were before we were married. We've become a whole new person by our union with another. Some may not want to take the name because of their reluctance to give up their old identity, but to be married is to find a new identity with the one we love that completes us in ways we had never known.

There are definite consequences and benefits to taking the name of our Husband. In John 15:21, Jesus is warning us that once we've taken His name, the world will hate us because we no longer belong to the world but belong to Him. He has already spoken of asking in His Name in John 14:13-14. My wife has a VISA card with my name on it just because we're married, and she can use it to buy whatever she needs. Once we've taken the name of Jesus and become His Bride, we have unlimited credit with Father.

John's Gospel of Love closes with a scene where Jesus asks the all-important question, not only of Peter, but of all who would follow Him, "Do you love Me more than these?" (John 21:15). The real question is, *"Do you love Me more than anything else in the world?"* If we love the former life more, we can't follow Jesus. If we love making money more, we can't follow Jesus. If we love mother or father or son or daughter or husband or wife more than we love Jesus, we cannot be His Bride. Jesus will not take second place to anything or anybody. He wants to be our Husband, and that means having first place in our lives.

10

His Body

Generally, when we speak of giving ourselves to the Lord, we say we give Him our heart, since such a decision is an act of the will, and the heart is the place where surrender is made. We also know that, through the new birth, our spirit has come alive so we can have communion with the Lord, who is Spirit. (See John 3:5-7; 4:24.) But can the Lord our Husband actually be interested in our body as well? And why do the Scriptures tell us to present our bodies as a living sacrifice to Him? (See Romans 12:1.)

True marriage—two becoming one—involves the giving of the total self to another. Openness, honesty, and the sharing of thoughts and ideas are required so two people can be of one mind. Similarly we express our feelings and emotions so our hearts become entwined. Since God Himself joins us together, there is also a spiritual union that enables a couple

117

to worship the Lord together as one. And finally there is what some have called "the act of marriage," where we give our body to the one we love. All of these aspects of love are important, and where any part is missing, the potential oneness that the couple could enjoy may not be realized.

No less is true in being the Bride of Christ. The Lord has given us His heart by freely choosing to lay down His life for us. We have His words to let us know His mind, so much so that we are told, "We *have* the mind of Christ" (1 Corinthians 2:16, author's italics)—we have it because He gave it to us. He has even given us of His Spirit; and on the Cross, the central symbol of Christianity, He gave us His body. When we are told to present our bodies as a living sacrifice to the Lord, to do so is merely our "reasonable" (Greek, *logiken*) service in light of what Christ has done for us. The Lord is just asking us to reciprocate.

The Scriptures even tell us that our body cannot fulfill its primary function apart from the Lord Jesus Christ. In 1 Corinthians 6:13 we read, "Yet the body is . . . *for the Lord*; and the *Lord is for the body.*" The main purpose of the body is *not* to consume food, experience pleasure, or attract members of the opposite sex, but rather to be a love gift to the Lord. And the Lord wants our body; He is *"for the body"*— He wants to express the beauty of His personality through our physical frame.

Although the body does need food in order to survive, food by itself is not sufficient to nourish us in the fullest sense of the word.

Jesus realized early in His ministry that "Man shall not live on bread alone" (Matthew 4:4). Quite literally, as a couple in love lives on the last words they received from the one who gives their life meaning, we too can live on the words of our Lover, the Lord Jesus. They sustain us as nothing else can. After feeding five thousand men plus women and children, our Lord pointed out the difference between food that perishes and "food which endures to eternal life . . ." (John 6:27). When asked for food that would never spoil, He said, "I *am* the bread of life" (John 6:35). Christ Himself is the ultimate food for which our body was created.

As our body was not fashioned just to eat physical food, neither was it made for immorality (1 Corinthians 6:13). There are many kinds of gluttons, and some people are never satisfied either with food or with a physical relationship. They always want more and more and more. Never being satisfied is not happiness, it's misery. It's like having a thousand hooks in your body all pulling in a different direction at once. It's the opposite of the completeness, contentment, and joy to be found in knowing Jesus. He's the love we've been looking for, and our body was made for Him.

Not only is our body made for the Lord, it is also intended to be eternal. We were made to live forever. If Adam and Eve had not sinned, blocking God's will for their lives, they'd still be alive today in their physical bodies. Unfortunately, they did sin, so the Lord provided the antidote for death in resurrection. The Scriptures tell us, "Now God has not only raised the Lord, but will also raise us up through His power" (1 Corinthians 6:14). What's the point of raising the Groom without raising the Bride?

The ideal of love is often expressed in the words, "And they lived happily ever after." Sadly, this is never the case in the natural order. Death always comes and takes our loved one away, and the marriage dissolves into a mist of memories. We have been separated in a very final way from the one we love. But there is a marriage that will go on forever and forever. The Bride and Bridegroom will both have eternal bodies, having been raised from the dead by the power of God.

Our union with Christ is for always, and once we have become one with Him by faith, we can never think of ourselves accurately as being apart from Him. In 1 Corinthians 6:15 we are asked, "Do you not know that *your bodies are members of Christ?*" We are permanently attached to Jesus just as our body is affixed to our head for life. This connection of the head to the body keeps us alive and empowers us to express our thoughts in actions.

As the various members of our body, our fingers and toes, arms and legs, are physical extensions of our body, even so are we to be physical extensions of Jesus. The Church is described in the Scriptures as *"His body,* the fulness of Him who fills all in all"* (Ephesians 1:22-23). "The fulness of Him" means *everything that Jesus is*, and this fulness is to be seen in us. Since Jesus has compassion, others should see His compassion at work in us. Since Jesus has all authority in heaven and earth, there should be evidence of that authority as we combat evil in the name above every name. Whatever Jesus is, He wants to be *in us*. He wants a physical presence on planet earth through us, the members of His Body.

Physical union in a marriage should be an outward sign of a much deeper union within. Where this inner union is missing, the physical act can become meaningless and even impossible. The Scripture speaks of this deeper union and says, "But the one who joins himself to the Lord is *one spirit with Him*" (1 Corinthians 6:17).

Our body is only the house we're living in. Our spirit is our truest self, our "innermost being" (see John 7:38), and it is in our spirit that we are one with Christ. For this reason, our oneness with Him is the greatest intimacy we can know. Jesus demonstrated this absolute oneness with Father when He rejoiced in the Holy Spirit (see Luke 10:21), communicating not just with His mind and His lips, but with His Spirit. This was real communion.

Obviously there are consequences to giving ourselves so completely to someone else. If we really give our body to them, *it belongs to them*, and we are accountable to them for how we use it. My wife cares about what I do with my body, because my body is now her body. She likes it when I get exercise and eat properly, taking care of my body. If I were to begin to do something harmful to my body, I have no doubt that she would try and stop me. She likes for me to dress up and look the best I can, because what I do with my body, which really belongs to her, reflects on her.

Jesus also cares about what we do with our body. For this reason we are told, "Flee immorality . . . the immoral man sins against his own body" (1 Corinthians 6:18), and "Therefore, glorify God in your body" (1 Corinthians 6:20). *It's His body now*, and we are to take good care of it, not doing the most harmful thing possible by being immoral, but using it to glorify Him.

Another result of giving our body to Him is becoming a temple of the Holy Spirit. Having established the fact that our bodies are members of Christ and we are one spirit with Him, we are asked, "Do you not know that your body is a temple of the Holy Spirit?" (1 Corinthians 6:19). The attitude of the question is one of surprise, as if to say, "Didn't you know that if the Lord Jesus comes to live in you, He'll want the Holy Spirit to come along as well?" Jesus lived His life here on earth by the power of the Holy Spirit. (See Luke 3:22; 4:1, 18.) He certainly does not want to leave the Holy Spirit behind when He comes to live in us.

In fact Jesus' death on the Cross was actually a preparation for our being filled with the Holy Spirit. *The Cross had to happen before Pentecost.* Our body was always intended to be a temple of the Holy Spirit; but the temple was dirty, contaminated with sin, so Jesus had to cleanse the temple. The Holy Spirit would never come into a person still defiled with sin (see John 14:17), so Jesus shed His blood to cleanse us from sin (see 1 John 1:7) *so we could be filled with the Holy Spirit.*

121

That Jesus poured out His life's blood for us tells us several things. It tells us how important it was to Jesus for us to literally become a temple of the Holy Spirit. In addition, we learn what value Jesus put upon us and our giving ourselves to Him body, soul, and spirit—the price He was willing to pay for us to be His Bride. And finally, we discover the answer to the question, "Who's body is it anyway?"

The Scripture reminds us in case we forget, "You have been bought with a price" (1 Corinthians 6:20), that price being the life of God the Son, that which held ultimate value in the universe. That's what was paid for us! Knowing this, can we ever doubt our worth or the worth of our brothers and sisters in Christ or that of those who could become members of His Body, His Bride, since *He died for all of us*?

For years I suffered with low self-esteem. I was convinced I was worthless, of no value to anyone. Self-destruction made a lot more sense than to continue living. The only thing that kept me alive was fear of the consequences of suicide. And then I discovered what Jesus says I'm worth. *God can't be wrong.* If Jesus says I'm worth dying for, *I must be.* The same is true for every person I meet. He died for them, too. We all have a value beyond our comprehension.

Some may imagine that their body belongs to them to do with as they wish. They think they have the right to destroy brain cells with alcohol and drugs, fill their lungs with nicotine, clog their arteries with cholesterol, and destroy a living fetus within them all because "It's my body!" But such thinking ignores the Word of the Lord that says, "Do you not know . . . *you are not your own? For you have been bought with a price*" (1 Corinthians 6:19-20). No one who is aware that Jesus died for them can continue to think in these terms. The price has been paid—Jesus shed His blood so we could be His Bride. Our body belongs to Him.

11

Undistracted Devotion

One of the greatest problems with marriages, at least in the United States, is maintaining the intimacy that was once enjoyed in the early days of the relationship. In the beginning, two people become "one"; but all too often in the end the "one" reverts back to "two" again, and they drift further and further apart.

This fact is especially sad when we realize just the opposite should and could be happening. In a healthy marriage the husband and wife can get closer and closer together as they share their lives more and more with the passing of time.

Saddest of all, this drifting apart can occur not only in our earthly marriages but in our union with the Lord as well. We've all known those whose love for the Lord has grown cold. We may even lack the passion we ourselves once had for Jesus. For this reason, Paul, inspired by the Holy Spirit, gives us several principles that will enable us to keep the intimacy alive in both our earthly and our heavenly marriage.

Single-minded devotion

The Scriptures state that our body belongs to the Lord and we are "one spirit with Him" (1 Corinthians 6:17). We have already come to know the Lord in an intimate way as prophesied by Jeremiah. (See Jeremiah 31:34.) However, we must remain single-minded in order to maintain that intimacy. Paul writes, "But because of immoralities, let each man have *his own* wife, and let each wife have *her own* husband" (1 Corinthians 7:2). Immorality is when we don't limit ourselves to the one person to whom we're married. Such infidelity can easily tear a marriage apart. Therefore, we are not to have a physical relationship with someone other than our own mate—we are to be faithful to *our own* wife or husband, *excluding all others.*

This choosing of one person to the exclusion of everyone else is the very thing that makes a deeper relationship possible. We are a "chosen" people and we have freely chosen to be the Bride of Christ. In doing so we have chosen NOT to be married to a million other things. Everything else is excluded. We belong to Christ alone.

Daydreaming about past loves or potential future ones is not a good way to get closer to your mate. Once we have made the choice, we are far better off to live by that commitment than to imagine it's never been made. Likewise, setting our mind on former worldly pleasures isn't likely to keep us close to Jesus. If we are wise, we will truly "set our mind on things above" because that's where Christ our Husband is (see Colossians 3:1-2).

One of the major temptations that I have in my walk with the Lord is what I call "distractions"—getting my mind on other things that cause me to neglect giving Him the attention He deserves. When I give in to this temptation, I find that I'm not as close to the Lord as I want to be, and all kinds of unpleasant consequences follow. Paul in his letter to the church at Corinth points us to something far better, *"undistracted devotion to the Lord."* (1 Corinthians 7:35).

Have you ever tried to talk seriously with someone you love when you didn't have their full attention? Maybe they were watching television or supper was on the stove— whatever the reason, they were distracted, at least temporarily. If so, do you remember how you felt? Most of us don't like being ignored, especially when we're pouring out our heart to someone we truly care about.

I'm convinced that the Lord would like to share His heart with us far more than we can imagine. After all, the object of all He's done for us is *to share life together.* Unfortunately, much of the time He can't get our attention. We're thinking about friends and family and our job and all the errands we need to run and a thousand other things, and if He does have something He wants to say to us, we aren't really listening. And listening is more than sitting through a Sunday School lesson or a sermon; it's truly hearing His voice in a very personal way, so that what we've heard changes us.

Most people are devoted to something or someone. We may be devoted to a club, to sports, to music, to our work, or our family. Occasionally we hear of a "devoted" father, mother, husband, or wife. Whatever we're devoted to has our attention. We may be distracted for a while, but our thoughts keep coming back to the thing or person we love the most. Eventually we may come to the place where we hardly think of anything else. We are completely caught up in the object of our desire. Jesus wants to be what our heart and mind keep returning to. He wants our undistracted devotion.

Fulfilling Our Duty

Along with this singleness of heart and mind, we need an awareness of our duties to the one we love if we would stay close to them. The Scripture continues, "Let the husband fulfill his *duty* to his wife, and likewise also the wife to her husband" (1 Corinthians 7:3). Duty is "what we owe," whether taxes or honor or love. Have you ever thought about *what you owe* to your marriage partner? We must owe something or the Scriptures would not use these terms. There are some things that only the wife can do for her husband and vice versa, and the Word of the Lord says *we owe it to them to fulfill those needs!*

Dr. Willard Harley, in his book, *His Needs, Her Needs,* spells out the things that our spouse needs us to do for them— the things that we owe to them. Just briefly, the husband owes it to his wife to give her affection, conversation, honesty, financial support, and family commitment. The wife owes it to her husband to grant him sexual fulfillment, recreational companionship, an attractive spouse, domestic support, and admiration. Where these needs are not met at home, there will be real temptation to have them met elsewhere. (See 1 Corinthians 7:5.) The Lord wants to lead us "around" temptation, not "into" it. Therefore, He commands us to fulfill these duties to our spouse.

The Lord our Husband is certainly committed to seeing that all the needs of His Bride are met. He knows we need affection, so He tells us to greet one another with a "holy kiss." (See Romans 16:16; 1 Corinthians 16:20; 2 Corinthians 13:12; 1 Peter 5:14.) Knowing our need to talk to Him, He invites us to "pray without ceasing" (1 Thessalonians 5:17). Understanding our need for honesty, He gives us the whole truth. (See John 16:13.) We have no fear of deprivation because we have the promise that all our needs will be supplied *in Christ Jesus.* (See Philippians 4:19.) We don't need to be anxious about our children in the faith since He has promised to finish the work He's started in them. (See Philippians 1:6.)

We can be certain that our perfect Husband will see that all our needs are met so we will be completely content with Him. But have you ever thought about what we owe Him or what He wants from us? In light of what He's done for us, *we owe Him everything and there are some specific things He wants from us.* As we have already seen, He wants children, or for us to "bear fruit" (John 15:1). He desires that we sing, dance, and make music in His presence as we celebrate His goodness. (See Psalm 150:3-6.) Worship belongs to Him, since He alone is worthy. (See Revelation 5:12.) His Bride is to be beautiful, holy, without spot or wrinkle (see Ephesians 5:27), and one who will share in His work, the work of the Kingdom.

Rejoicing

Though there are several duties that a husband and wife owe to one another, when Paul writes, "Stop depriving one another, except by agreement for a time that you may devote yourselves to prayer . . . " (1 Corinthians 7:5), he is referring to the sexual relationship. According to this Scripture, to neglect this very important aspect of intimacy is wrong. The one acceptable cause for depriving one another is *in order to spend that time in prayer.*

The Lord wants us to find fulfillment in a holy, wholesome sexual relationship. Otherwise, why would He make us the way He did? When a couple's dating, one of the reasons they decide to get married is because they are physically attracted to one another, and that attraction should continue throughout their married life. It's one of the things that binds them together and makes them "one." For this reason husbands are told, "Rejoice in the wife of your youth . . . Be exhilarated always with her love" (Proverbs 5:18-19). The suggestion here is that the couple is no longer young, but they can still be attracted to each other.

Since this is the command of the Lord, we must not fail to continue delighting in our mate. Not surprisingly, there are tragic results when we ignore the will of the Lord in this regard. Can you imagine being the person who was once attractive to your spouse, knowing you aren't any more? Being appealing to a person of the opposite sex is an important part of our self-esteem, and that person should be our marriage partner. When this is not the case, the daily rejection can become almost unbearable. The person feeling the rejection may harden their heart toward the person they once loved and look for someone who does find them attractive.

This principle for intimacy is so important that the Scriptures allow only one exception when we may abstain, ". . . that you may devote yourselves to prayer" (1 Corinthians 7:5). The only valid reason for not being intimate with your wife or husband is in order to get closer to the Lord and be intimate with Him. Notice that nothing is mentioned about a headache or a hard day or what kind of mood we're in. This is the right thing to do and the loving thing to do, and love doesn't come and go with the breeze.

If not rejoicing in our earthly partner is wrong, how much worse must it be to not "rejoice in the Lord always" (Philippians 4:4)? Do we imagine we can neglect our worship of Him who is everything good and beautiful and stay just as close to Him? Worship is our main function as the Bride of Christ (see Luke 10:42), and we only have true joy when we're rejoicing in Him who is the source of all our joy. Unfortunately, even this aspect of our partnership with Jesus can be crowded out by too much activity. Thus we are warned against "*Forsaking* our own assembling together" for worship (Hebrews 10:25), especially since we know the Day of the Lord is approaching, and we want to be as close to Him as we can be when He returns.

Rejoicing in the Lord is not to be sporadic any more than rejoicing in the wife of our youth. We are to rejoice in the Lord "*always*" (see Philippians 4:4). That means our rejoicing doesn't depend on our mood or pleasant circumstances or immediate answers to prayer or anything else. Regardless of all these other things, *the Lord is still the Lord, and we're His Bride. He is worthy of our worship. He desires our worship. If we really want to stay close to Him, we will worship.*

Commitment

The next essential ingredient for intimacy is commitment. We must be in this relationship "for keeps" from the very beginning. Here our instructions from the Lord are "that a wife should not leave her husband" and "that the husband should not send his wife away" (see 1 Corinthians 7:10-11). Those who get married "looking for the back door" should not be surprised when the marriage doesn't work. *Practicallly nothing does work with an attitude like that.* If we are prepared to quit the moment we encounter difficulties, we should not expect to meet with much success.

Marriage is to be a permanent arrangement for our own good and because that's the way love works. Love doesn't quit. The love chapter tells us, "Love [Greek, *agape*] endures all things . . . never fails [gives up, quits]" (1 Corinthians 13:7-8). This, of course, is the God kind of love that's required to build a marriage and not the unstable romantic kind that we hear so much about. When things aren't going their way, a person with the God kind of love has already made up their mind, "I'm not leaving—I'll will do whatever it takes to work through this problem." This person is a winner, both in marriage and in many other areas of their life.

Christ our Husband clearly demonstrates this type of love for us. He says to His Bride, "I will *never* desert you, nor will I *ever* forsake you" (Hebrews 13:5). Christ's commitment to us is what gives us certainty about our salvation. No doubt our Lord is not always perfectly pleased with our words and our behavior. Nevertheless, He does not abandon us, but keeps on loving us, helping us to grow in love ourselves. But He expects us to have the same type of commitment toward Him. Knowing we will experience situations that could cause us to stop loving Him, He says, "It is the one who has endured to the end who will be saved" (Matthew 10:22). Our salvation, spending eternity with Him in glory, actually depends upon our persistence in loving Him, even when to fall away and deny Him might be easier. To truly love the Lord is to love to the end *no matter what*

Flexibility

Another important part of maintaining intimacy is a willingness to change. The Holy Spirit speaks through Paul and says, "The unbelieving husband is sanctified [made holy] through his wife, and the unbelieving wife is sanctified through her believing husband . . ." (1 Corinthians 7:14). Being changed from unbelieving and "unholy" to "holy" is a major change, but we have all seen a spouse make this transition because of the godly example of their wife or husband. Had they not been married to a believer, this change probably would not have happened.

Marriage often causes seemingly impossible changes to occur in one or both partners. Up until the time that my wife and I were married, I had never eaten broccoli or asparagus; or if I had, I didn't like it! Marsha, on the other hand, loved both. Needless to say, I've learned to like broccoli and asparagus. On the other hand, Marsha didn't care for Dr. Pepper before we were married; but after seeing how much I enjoy good, cold Dr. Peppers, she's developed a taste for them, too.

One of the most wonderful things about being one with Christ is the fact that we are changed by that union. Since He is holy, we become holy. We call this change "salvation."

But even after the New Birth, we continue to be changed. As we gaze upon His glory, we become like Him. The more we "gaze" or spend time seeking His face, the more we're changed. The Scripture says concerning His Bride, "We all . . . beholding as in a mirror the glory of the Lord, *are being transformed into the same image from glory to glory . . .*" (2 Corinthians 3:18).

Living to Please

The final secret for success in maintaining intimacy is living to please the one we love. Once again the Holy Spirit speaks through Paul and says, "One who is married is concerned about . . . how he may please his wife, and . . . how she may please her husband" (1 Corinthians 7:33-34). According to this Scripture, *to be married is to live to please the one you love.* Why would you marry a person in the first place if you didn't want to make them happy?

There are literally millions of people who would love to find someone who would live to bring them joy. Some have never married, some are divorced, and some are married. If they could discover such a person, they would marry them immediately and live with them "happily ever after." No one could reasonably leave someone whose one desire was to make them happy.

Earlier we mentioned "undistracted devotion" (1 Corinthians 7:35) and singleness of mind and heart. The single motivation here is to please the one we love. That is "devotion." "Undistracted devotion" is continually approaching the one we love with the question, "What can I do for you?" instead of the demand, "Here's what I want you to do for me." The first attitude is one of love, the second is one of selfishness. Constantly making demands can tear down a relationship, while thoughtful giving builds bonds that are hard to break.

Concerning Christ's attitude toward us, the Scripture says, "He is able to save forever those who draw near to God through Him, since *He always lives to make intercession for them.*" (Hebrews 7:25). The picture here is the Lord our Husband constantly waiting to hear our needs and desires expressed so He can make sure they are fulfilled. This is His full-time preoccupation, since He "always lives" to do it. We cannot imagine what all He wants to do for His Bride. His resources are unlimited and His willingness is obvious. He has promised to give us the desires of our heart if we will delight in Him. (See Psalm 37:4.) Knowing this, how could we ever consider leaving Him and "falling away"?

Our reasonable response to this kind of love is to live to please Him as well. The Psalmist expressed what we feel toward Our Lord and Master when he wrote, "I delight to do your will" (Psalm 40:8). The thing that gives us joy more than anything else is to please Him and do His will. The writer of Hebrews refers to this Scripture and then says, "By this will we have been sanctified" (see Hebrews 10:7, 9, 10). This attitude of living to please the Lord is the very thing that sanctifies (sets us apart as belonging to Him). The person who doesn't want to do His will is not married to Him in their heart. We know we belong to Him because we want to do His will. (See 1 John 2:3-6.)

As the Lord lives to grant our desires and we delight to do His will, we experience completed love and the joy that marriage was intended to be. Nothing is sadder than incomplete love where one person wants to rejoice in the other one, but the feeling is not mutual. But when two people have pleasing the other person as their one desire, heaven has arrived. The reason heaven is such a joyful place is because it has always been a place of complete unselfishness and always will be. But we can have that joy right here on earth. Christ came to give us His joy. He taught us how to love. He called us to be His Bride.

12

The Great Mystery

I've always loved a mystery. Every time a new Sherlock Holmes mystery comes on television, I tape it. I like to try and figure out the ending, the "whodunnit." Sometimes I'm successful, sometimes I'm not. God is the author of the greatest mystery of all time. He's been telling a story with a secret ending for a very long time. Finally in these "last days" (Hebrews 1:2), He has revealed how things are going to ultimately turn out. *We who believe on Jesus are going to be His Bride throughout eternity.* This has always been the plan of God and it shall come to pass.

Paul wrote about this mystery in his letter to the church at Ephesus. Inspired by the Holy Spirit, he gave extensive instructions about how a husband and wife can find fulfillment in marriage, and then added, "This *mystery* is great; but *I am speaking with reference to Christ and the church.*" (Ephesians 5:32). The mystery of history is the fact that everything God's been doing since the beginning of time was leading up to obtaining a Bride for His Son. This purpose is the focal point of His salvation.

Two truths summarize the contents of this passage: *Christ is the head of the Church*, and *Christ loves the Church*. In one sense they are two halves of the same truth, and one is incomplete without the other. Paul begins his description of our marriage to Christ by saying, "The husband is the head of the wife as Christ also is the head of the church" (Ephesians 5:23), and "The church is subject to Christ" (Ephesians 5:24). Christ's relationship to us is "He's the Head"; our relationship to Christ is "we're subject to Him."

Christ is not "one of the heads," along with the pastor or pastors, various committees and boards, and domineering personalities within the congregation. He's the only head. A body with more than one head is a monstrosity. I've never seen a body with two heads, but I can imagine the difficulty of having two brains sending messages to the body at the same time. With each additional head or extra signal from a brain the confusion and frustration would be complicated even further.

There's only one head for the Body of Christ, and His name is Jesus. You and I are not the head, and we dare not try and usurp His position. If we are in the Body at all, we're "subject to" Him. We become His Body and His Bride by confessing Him as Lord (see Romans 10:9), saying we will gladly receive direction from Him. We can no more be joined to Jesus without this attitude than we can join the army determined to disobey all orders. Any part of the body not receiving signals from the head is dead, useless, and soon to be cut off. On the other hand, when we are all getting directions from the Lord our Husband, the confusion that comes from trying to have many "heads" disappears, and there is peace and harmony.

To be "subject to" Christ is simply to be responsive to His leadership as the body is responsive to the head. The various parts of the body do not debate whether or not they will obey the nerve impulses sent from the brain. When the signal comes, the appropriate action results. So it is with the Body of Christ. We await His commands, and go when He says "go."

Having Christ as our head is definitely to our advantage. As such He is also "The Savior of the body" (Ephesians 5:23). When Jesus is our head or Lord, He is also our Savior. Over and over again He is called, "Our Lord *and* Savior Jesus Christ." The two titles go together. Nowhere in the New Testament are we presented with two options, "Lord" *or* "Savior." If He is Lord, then He is Savior; if He is Savior, then He is Lord. He cannot save us without our being willing to follow Him any more than Moses could have saved the Israelites from bondage had they not followed him out of Egypt.

When we recognize Him as our Lord and head, He saves us, not only from the confusion we mentioned earlier, but also from slavery to the evil one and selfishness. To yield to Christ as our head is to no longer have Satan as our head and to be set free from the self-centered life that he inspires. Our will now belongs to Jesus. He's the head, and we're the body; He's the Savior, and we're liberated to love and serve Him.

Another advantage to having Christ as our head is the actual direction He gives. *We need to know which way to go* and His will is always for our good. Without His leadership, we're all like sheep gone astray (Isaiah 53:6) and will bring about our own destruction. Knowing His will, we know the path to safety and blessing.

Jesus is our head by virtue of who He is. He is the Christ, the King of kings and Lord of lords. But He deserves our being subject to Him for still another reason: *He loves us.* Paul continues, "Christ also loved the church and gave Himself up for her" (Ephesians 5:25).

How foolish we would be to yield our will to a person bent on our destruction instead of one who desired only the very best for us. And yet, when we sin—give in to the will of Satan—that's exactly what we do. Jesus, on the other hand, wants to give us the abundant life, and, unlike Satan, is worthy of our trust.

Paul goes into great detail about the love of the Lord that compels us to want to follow Him. He reminds us of the greatest act of love in history when Jesus died on the Cross for us, His Bride, "[He] gave Himself up for her" (Ephesians 5:25). Here he defines what love truly is, giving one's self up for another or laying down our life for them. (See John 15:13). Jesus death on the Cross showed us the real meaning of love. Surely we can learn to rely upon love like this.

Any husband who daily "lays down his life" for his wife will have little trouble gaining her confidence. She will know from the outset that any suggestions he makes are only for her well-being and to make her happy and will consider his advice very carefully. The same principle applies with the Bride of Christ. Knowing the proven love of the Lord, we want to hear His voice.

Every one of us who is married has the choice to make whether we will love with the love of Christ or not. We will either "give ourselves up" for the one we love or we will yield to the temptation offered Jesus on the Cross and "save ourselves" (see Matthew 27:40). Couples who have turned to "saving themselves" and looking out for their own interests cannot be happy for very long since selfishness is not a good foundation for marriage. But those who choose to follow Christ, in looking out for the interests of another, even to the point of refusing to save their own life, are well on their way to a beautiful marriage where two people have faith in each other.

The Lord wants His love to engender trust in His Bride. There are also several other effects He wants His love to have in the life of His Beloved. After telling us that Christ has demonstrated His love by giving Himself up for us, the Scripture continues, ". . . that He might sanctify her" (Ephesians 5:26). This is the purpose for Christ doing what He did and the desired result for which He's looking.

Love should make a difference in our lives. Often love can make a person who was previously irresponsible into a responsible person, a person who never thought of others into a more sensitive person, or a poor student into a good student. We should be better, stronger, and more fulfilled because of the union we have formed with another.

Three Little Words

Surely our being joined to Jesus will make us a better person. Three words describe the new you and the new me once we have become His Bride: *sanctified, holy,* and *blameless.* (See Ephesians 5:26-27.)

Sanctified

Christ gave Himself up for His Bride "that He might *sanctify* her" (Ephesians 5:26, author's italics). Jesus wants a sanctified bride. Sanctification basically involves two things, getting clean and belonging to the Lord instead of the evil one. To explain a part of what Jesus did to sanctify his Bride, the Scripture says, "*Having cleansed her* by the washing of water with the word" (Ephesians 5:26, author's italics). Through proclamation of the gospel that we received with faith, and water baptism symbolizing true repentance, we have been cleansed from sin. We're no longer a "dirty" bride.

A person is either dirty or clean. We've either washed our hands before dinner or we haven't. We've either been cleansed from sin or we haven't been, and 1 John 1:9 says that every true believer has been so cleansed.

Faith says the atoning death of Christ paid the full penalty for sin so we could be forgiven, and the change of heart called repentance takes care of the rebellious nature that caused us to sin in the first place. The Lord truly does "cleanse us from *ALL* unrighteousness" just like He said He would.

The other aspect of sanctification is belonging to the Lord. We *were* in bondage to Satan through sin; we willingly chose to serve him, and as a result, we belonged to him. But now that the sin problem has been solved and we have been redeemed by the blood of the Lamb, we choose to live for the Lord Jesus Christ, and by virtue of that choice, *we belong to Him.*

We belong to the Lord because we gave ourselves to Him. If I gave you a watch, it would become your watch the moment you received it. The same would be true of a car, cash, or even myself. By the very act of giving, a transfer of ownership is made. Marriage is the act of giving ourselves to someone else. If we have given ourselves to the Lord, we're *His* Bride.

When we offer our life to Jesus, He has promised to never turn us away, "The one who comes to Me, I will certainly not cast out" (John 6:37). To present ourselves is to be received, and to be received is to belong to Him. On another occasion Jesus said, "The altar . . . *sanctifies* the offering" (Matthew 23:19). The altar is the place where we present our life to the Lord and the place where we become *completely His.* Once the sacrifice of ourselves has been placed upon His altar, the offering is sanctified.

Even better than our belonging to Him is the fact that He belongs to us. Has He not given Himself to us also? Have we not received Him? If so, then He is in truth, *"Our* Lord and Savior Jesus Christ." When we gave ourselves to Him, we gave Him every part of our lives; our heart, soul, mind, and strength; and our fears, faults, and failures. In the same way, He has given Himself to us completely, including His righteousness, wisdom, name, and nature. All that He is and has is ours. We belong to each other.

Holy

The Lord loved us the way He did in order to sanctify us and to make us holy and blameless. As further explanation of why Jesus loved the Church and gave Himself up for her, Paul writes, " . . . that He might present to Himself the church in all her glory . . . that she should be holy and blameless" (Ephesians 5:27). "Holy" means "like the Lord." This term is often used in contrast with human nature since we are anything but "holy" without Christ. The unregenerate man is selfish while the Lord is giving; he has a tendency to lie while the Lord is truth. When we look at ourselves before the new birth, we conclude, "God's not like us. He is holy."

But the gospel of Jesus Christ tells us *we can be changed and become like Him.* Why else would He tell us, "Be holy, for I am holy" (1 Peter 1:16)? When Jesus died on the Cross, He did so to make us holy (*"that* she should be *holy"*). The Cross of Christ accomplished everything it was supposed to. If Jesus died to make us holy, then we're holy.

The word "glory" is closely related to being holy. Glory has to do with all the brightness and beauty that is the Lord. The glory of a flower is what's beautiful about a flower, and the glory of a baby is what's beautiful about the baby. Likewise, the glory of the Lord is what's beautiful about Him, what attracts us to Him; and He wants us to share His glory. He wants to "present to Himself the church in all her *glory"* (Ephesians 5:27).

We have no glory apart from Him, but we can reflect His glory as in a mirror. This change from having no glory to having His glory is His work alone. The Lord is going to *"present to Himself"* the Church in glory. Like a man who takes an old clunker of a car, rebuilds the motor, refinishes the body, making it a thing of beauty, and then presents his own work to himself as a gift so that he is delighted with the finished product; even so, the Lord takes us as we are, reshapes us into His likeness, and then presents us to Himself as a gift so that He is completely pleased with what He's done with us.

Blameless

Christ makes us holy and thereby enables us to reflect His glory. But how do we become "blameless?" He wants us to be blameless, too. Being blameless is being able to say truthfully, "It's not my fault." Most children would like for parents to believe this is their perpetual state of being. No matter what happens, "It's not my fault!" The implication may be, "I'm not responsible; you're the parent, you're in charge, and regardless of what kind of mess was made, the responsibility lies with you."

Are we responsible for our own lives? Some would say with the poet that they are the master of their fate, the captain of their soul. If so, whatever goes wrong, *it's their fault.* They are *not blameless* if they're responsible. But suppose someone else really was in charge and the ultimate outcome actually was someone else's responsibility? *Then we could be blameless.* If we are still holding the reins of our life, trying to be in control, then we cannot possibly know what it means to be blameless. But if we have turned those reins over to another, the Lord our Husband, and what we become is up to Him, then we are truly blameless.

The Scriptures tell us what the Lord expects to happen to us as a result of His giving Himself up for us. They also describe for us His ongoing love that is with us every day. The passage continues, "No one ever hated his own flesh, but nourishes and cherishes it, *just as Christ also does the church*" (Ephesians 5:29, author's italics).

To nourish one's self is to make sure the body has everything it needs to be strong and healthy. Christ nourishes the Church as an expression of His love for the Church. He wants us strong and healthy. *Whatever we need today in order to be strong, He wants us to have it.* He instructs us in His Word, "Finally, be strong in the Lord and in the strength of *His* power" (Ephesians 6:10). Whatever power He has is ours in order to make us mighty. He gives us weapons that are "divinely powerful for the destruction of fortresses" (2 Corinthians 10:4), such as prayer and the name above every name. Many times in the Scriptures we are told, "Be strong and courageous" (Joshua 1:6-7), and the Lord gives us the courage we require. Often courage means the difference between victory and defeat. If we are fearful, we will flee; but if we are courageous, the enemy will run away in terror. Jesus has never been afraid of anything or anybody, and He gives His courage to us.

As nourishing our spouse is an expression of love for them, so is cherishing them. When we cherish someone or something, we treat that person or thing as having great value. For example, cherished memories are memories beyond value. There are some things we really can't put a price on. The other day I asked a friend what he would pay in order to save his life or the life of a loved one. His answer was in essence, "Whatever it took." We cannot put a value on a human life and treat it as expendable even when it's socially or economically inconvenient. Human beings are beyond value; we can't put a price on them.

If we are married, our spouse is a person to be cherished and treated as a gift from the Lord worth more than all the money in the world. The excellent wife of Proverbs is described in this way, "Her worth is far above jewels" (Proverbs 31:10), which tells us a man is foolish to spend all of his time making money if he neglects his wife who is worth more than money. Inspired by the Holy Spirit, Paul writes these instructions to the wife, "Let the wife see that she respects and reverences her husband, that she notices him, regards him, honors him, prefers him, venerates and esteems him; and that she defers to him, praises him, and loves and admires him exceedingly" (Ephesians 5:33, AMP). Can you imagine a home where the wife treated her husband the way the Lord says she should and where the husband gave his wife the value the Lord says she actually has? Who wouldn't want to be part of such a household? We can be, if we follow the Lord's direction together.

Christ our Husband always cherishes us, treating us as if we are worth more than we could possibly imagine. Having this estimation of us, He couldn't dismiss His disciples for their constant failures; nor can He dismiss us. He has already decided we're worth whatever it takes to get us where we're supposed to be, even dying on a Cross. Having paid the ultimate price for us, *He will not give up on us somewhere along the way.*

To further emphasize the permanence of His love, Paul concludes with a reference to the original institution of marriage in the Garden of Eden as a picture of our relationship to Christ. He writes, "Two shall become one flesh. This mystery is great; for I am speaking with reference to Christ and the church" (Ephesians 5:31-32; see also Genesis 2:24). For ages, the mystery that the Son of God wanted a bride to love, to sanctify and make holy and blameless, to nourish and cherish continually, was hidden to humanity. Now the mystery is revealed. We can now understand the ultimate purpose of God. What remains a mystery is why He should love us so, why He should place such a value on us and give Himself so completely to us. Perhaps we will understand in eternity. Perhaps that's just the mystery of love.

13

A Holy Bride

When I was growing up, purity was something that was greatly appreciated and encouraged. A man expected his bride to be pure, and girls who were known to have loose morals were to be avoided. Through the influence of movies and television, much of our moral thinking has changed. We are made to believe that to be a virgin is to be unwanted, that there's no reason to wait until you're married to have sex, and that "everybody's doing it." The outcome of such thinking includes the extreme weakening of a bond that helps hold a marriage together, rampant social diseases, and an instability in our nation that we have never known before due to the disintegration of the family.

In spite of popular opinion, God's standard has not changed. He still wants a holy Bride. In fact, a holy Bride is the only type of bride He will have. Many of the Scriptures concerning the Lord's search for a Bride depict a broken heart due to the impurity of the one whom He loved. Israel was rejected for her unfaithfulness; and the Lord turned to the nations, determined to find a bride that was faithful, pure, and holy.

An Adulterous People

The weeping prophet, Jeremiah, spoke for the Lord to register His disappointment in the way His people had responded to His love. One of the saddest Scriptures in the Bible is found in Jeremiah 3:14, which reads, "Return . . . for I am Lord and Master and Husband to you . . ." (AMP). I can only imagine the pain of being abandoned for someone else by the one you love. No doubt the pain would be in proportion to the love of the one left behind. None of us can fully comprehend the love of the Lord for us; it's simply too great. Nor can we completely know His broken heart when we reject Him.

The people of the Lord had gone after other lovers by following the surrounding nations into idolatry. They wanted to "fit in" with those around them instead of being "holy unto the Lord." Therefore, the Lord said to them, "You are a harlot with many lovers" (Jeremiah 3:1b). An idol is anything we place above our relationship with the Lord. Apparently Judah had put many things ahead of the Lord in trying to be like her neighbors. Consequently, she could no longer enjoy the blessings of wedded bliss. The Lord explained the effect of her unfaithfulness in this way, "Therefore, the showers have been withheld, and there has been no spring rain" (Jeremiah 3:3). Rain was a sign of blessing; when the rain was withheld, Judah was no longer in the place of blessing.

Take A Number

Couples who consistently put work, the children, recreation, or some other interest ahead of loving each other will not know the joy the Lord intends us to have in marriage. The blessing of just being together will slowly slip away until they suddenly wake up and wonder what happened.

Churches that have not really experienced the blessing of the Lord for a very long time should take a word of warning from this passage. The reason could be that with all our activity we have actually put other things ahead of knowing the Lord. Martha made the mistake of doing housework when she could have been sitting at the feet of Jesus. (See Luke 10:38-42.) The Pharisees substituted the Law for loving the Lord. But there are no better plans than being in the presence of Jesus, and nothing and no one else deserves first place in our lives.

I Did It My Way

The dangers of making our own plans apart from the Lord are pointed out in this chapter. Speaking to His people, His wife, the Lord says, *"You have had your way"* (Jeremiah 3:5). Sometimes having our own way is the most harmful thing that could happen. For the sake of peace a husband or wife might consistently give in to the wishes of their mate and yet be truly hurt knowing the one they love so much doesn't care about their desires or feelings.

The same situation can happen within a church. One or more members within the Body of Christ can insist on always having their own way and the rest of the congregation go along with them just to keep peace; but the Lord will not be pleased that His will was not considered, and more often than not, the church will begin to die both spiritually and numerically. We can truly hurt the Lord by having our way so that He eventually removes the candlestick of His presence from our midst. (See Revelation 2:5.)

The Divorce of a Nation

According to the prophet, the Lord was so hurt by Israel that He gave her a divorce. Speaking for the Lord, he writes, "For all the adulteries of faithless Israel I had sent her away and *given her a writ of divorce*" (Jeremiah 3:8). Even with the Lord, there comes a time when enough is enough, when He knows we will never respond to His love, and He ceases to draw us to Himself. He warns us, "My Spirit shall not strive with man forever" (Genesis 6:3). We cannot safely continue to spurn His love and presume upon His mercy.

The main point of this Scripture is to stop the people of the Lord before they get to the point of no return. He is still calling out to them in love, even with a broken heart, "Return, faithless Israel . . . for I am gracious . . . Return, O faithless sons, I will heal your faithlessness" (Jeremiah 3:12, 22). The original hearers of this call did not return and experience the healing promised here. Instead they were taken away captive into Babylon. If we can hear this call from the Lord today, it's not too late for us.

Jeremiah was not the only prophet to express the grief of the Lord over His Beloved. Ezekiel also contrasted the perfect love of the Lord with the very imperfect love of His Bride. He began by telling how the Lord had made an offer of marriage to the descendants of Abraham. In Ezekiel 16:8 he wrote, "I spread My skirt over you . . . and entered into a covenant with you so that you became Mine. . . ." This expression of belonging, of covenant relationship, is clearly a picture of marriage, so any lack of faithfulness would constitute adultery.

The Lord continues to speak of His love through the prophet, "I also clothed you with . . . fine linen . . . silk . . . bracelets . . . a necklace . . . a ring . . . your beauty . . . was perfect *because of My splendor which I bestowed on you . . .*" (Ezekiel 16:10-14). The Lord wanted to give His splendor, His glory, and His nature to His Bride. But her reaction to such an incredible offer was far less than satisfactory, "But you trusted in *your* beauty and played the harlot . . ." Ezekiel 16:15). To trust in our own righteousness instead of receiving the free gift of the righteousness of Christ by faith is to be *unfaithful*. It is to join ourselves to something else for what we need and to play the harlot spiritually. Such behavior comes from pride and independence.

Town Between Two Lovers

Naturally, the Lord decries such unfaithfulness. He speaks to the one He would have given everything and says, "You adulteress wife, who takes strangers instead of her husband!" (Ezekiel 16:32). The Lord of love has been cast aside for other lovers. Who can know His pain?

I wish I could say that such Scriptures are limited to the Old Testament, but in the Epistle of James we find similar language addressed to "the brethren." After explaining that our prayers may not be answered because of wrong motives, the brother of the Lord writes, "You adulteresses, do you not know that friendship with the world is hostility toward God? Therefore, whoever wishes to be a friend of the world makes himself an enemy of God" (James 4:4).

Is the Church really torn between two lovers, trying to love the Lord on one hand and the world on the other? If so, we may rest assured that such a strategy *will not work*. The Lord will not share His Bride with another. We will either abandon the world with its passions and desires for the joy of knowing Jesus, or we will betray our Lord with unfaithfulness and make ourselves His enemy.

I have counseled those who have been betrayed by a marriage partner who committed adultery, and in every case there was a mountain of either hurt or anger or both that was nearly impossible to overcome. In some cases, through forgiveness and a total rebuilding of the trust that had been destroyed, the marriage was saved. But in no case did the spouse continue to be unfaithful and the marriage survive. Where there was healing, there was also genuine repentance and a willingness to start over together.

If we have been wedded to the world while claiming to be the Lord's Beloved, the time has come to repent, to change our ways, and give ourselves totally to Him. We have offended Him in the worst way possible, but He will forgive if we turn from impurity and love Him with all our heart (2 Chronicles 7:14).

Repent

The Scriptures make it clear that if we do not repent of our adulterous ways, we will not be acceptable when Christ returns. He's coming for a Bride "having no spot or wrinkle or any such thing . . . holy [pure] and blameless" (Ephesians 5:27). "Having no spot" means having nothing inconsistent with love such as envy, hatred, or unforgiveness. "Having no wrinkle" means having no darkness in our lives, having nothing contrary to the glory of the Lord.

The Lord our Husband is determined that His glory will be seen in us. We see the finished product of all He has planned in the last book of the Bible. John saw the culmination of history (which is actually *His story*) and the realization of the goal toward which our Lord is always moving, and recorded what he saw for us. In the last two chapters of Revelation, he portrayed the Church, the Bride in all her glory. He introduced the Bride by saying, "And I saw the holy city, new Jerusalem, coming down out of heaven from God, *made ready as a bride adorned for her husband.*" (Revelation 21:2, author's italics). He continued to emphasize the fact that he was talking about the Bride when he wrote, "And one of the seven angels . . . came and spoke with me, saying, 'Come here, *I shall show you the bride, the wife of the Lamb*' " (Revelation 21:9, author's italics).

I will never forget the beauty of my bride when I first saw her on our wedding day. When she entered the chapel of First Baptist Church in Oxford, Mississippi, I knew I'd never seen anything so radiant in my entire life. When the Lord sent a message to John through His angel, having seen His Bride in the beauty of holiness, I believe the feeling was much the same, only multiplied many times over. If the Lord had been wearing a vest, every button would have popped off. He had viewed us in the glory yet to be revealed, and He couldn't help telling us how wonderful we looked to Him. This was the Bride for which He had been waiting.

We Have His Glory and Nature

He began by saying we have His glory. (See Revelation 21:11.) There is no greater glory than the glory of the Lord, and He imparts His beauty to us. Michelangelo may or may not have been handsome outwardly; but he had a beauty in his soul that could transform a piece of marble into a creation of incredible wonder. In "The Battle Hymn of the Republic" we sing that Christ has "a glory in His bosom that transfigures you and me." He is in truth "making all things new" (Revelation 21:5).

Since holiness and love are inseparable, He told us, "The city was pure gold" (Revelation 21:18). Pure gold is gold that's been through the fire, and pure love is love that's been tested. It's love that held when we experienced rejection, ridicule, betrayal, and men saying all manner of evil against us falsely for His sake. (See Matthew 5:11.) We're being purified and our love is being perfected. Therefore, we really can rejoice. (See Matthew 5:12.) The Lord is doing His work in us.

Because we have His glory and His nature, which is love, He acknowledged us as His wife by saying, "His name shall be on their foreheads" (Revelation 22:4). Like a stamp of ownership, He has placed His Name upon us to declare to heaven and earth that we belong to Him. The evil one has his mark upon those who are his, and Jesus has His Name upon those purchased with His blood.

Having the Name of the Bridegroom means we are married to Him—we are one with Him. What we do, we do together. If Jesus, having died to sin and having been raised from the dead, is seated in heavenly places at Father's right hand, the place of power, then we, crucified with Him and raised to newness of life, are seated there with Him. (See Ephesians 2:4-6.) If the Governor lives in the Governor's mansion, his wife lives there with him. When the President of the United States moves into the White House, his wife accompanies him. And when Christ, the King of kings and Lord of lords, ascends to the ultimate place of power in the universe, He takes His Bride with Him to be by His side. (See Ephesians 4:8; John 14:3.)

Fulfilling Our Destiny

Having the name above every name and our position in Christ enables us to carry out the function for which we were created, the function the first Adam gave up without a whimper. (See Genesis 1:26; Psalm 8:6.) Concerning the time when His Bride would finally fill her place, the Lord spoke through His messenger, "They shall reign forever and ever" (Revelation 22:5). How different from the harlot wallowing in shame is the wife of the Lamb reigning with Him in glory.

God created a wife for man to work with him and be "a helper suitable for him" (Genesis 2:18). As the wife of the Lamb, you and I will work with Him throughout eternity seeing that His will is done in the new heaven and the new earth. Having learned the obedience of meekness, we'll inherit the earth. (See Matthew 5:5.) Having learned to submit to the Lord's authority here, we will be given authority to reign with Him in His everlasting kingdom.

Even So, Lord Jesus, Come

The last note of this revelation of Jesus Christ and His Bride, the Church, sounds almost like two turtledoves cooing to one another. Each is calling out to the other, "Come, come." The record reads, "The Spirit and the bride say, 'Come.' And let the one who hears say, 'Come.' And let the one who is thirsty come . . . Come, Lord Jesus" (Revelation 22:17, 20). The true Bride can hardly wait for her Husband to return. The best thing that could possibly happen would be for Him to come back today. With every beat of her heart she says, "Come, Lord Jesus." But the heart of the Lord is also calling out to a Bride not yet prepared for His return, still living in unfaithfulness, without the purity of heart that's required, not submitting to His Lordship so she can reign with Him. He says to the one who is *thirsty for the intimate relationship with Him that's still lacking*, "Let the one who is thirsty come." He wants every one of us to be a part of His Bride when He returns.

Jesus is coming back for one purpose and one purpose only: to claim a holy Bride without spot or wrinkle. Like a husband who's been away a long time making preparations for his wife to be with him, our Lord assures us, "I am coming quickly [soon]" (Revelation 22:20). As Beloved is anxious for His return, our Lover also anticipates the day when love will know its fullness, when everything that separates will be abolished, and we'll be reunited with the One for whom we were created, the Lord our Husband.